Just Between You, Me, and the Fence Post

By
Roger Setterdahl

*"We live by faith,
not by sight."*

2 Corinthians 5:7

Trafford rev. 11/09/2021

Trafford PUBLISHING® www.trafford.com

North America & international
toll-free: 844-688-6899 (USA & Canada)
fax: 812 355 4082

Introduction

How can the content of this book be described? Is it a mixture of thoughts gleaned from various parts of the Bible? Is it a hodge_podge of information that the Author tries to convey to the reader? Is it nothing more than a scrapbook that contains ideas and experiences? Perhaps it is a collection of mistaken perceptions that has no real place in the world today! Perhaps this book amounts to nothing and deserves to be filed in the trash can immediately. Whatever may be the reader's thoughts about this book and previous books that I've written, I offer no apologies. If the reader has been offended, I want you to know that was not my intention, but I do offer blunt assessments of the religious community as I perceive it to be. Realize that I write from my own perspective, my own personal experiences, and my own personal beliefs, however right or wrong they may be in some else's eyes. I do not encourage anyone to believe as I do. Everyone is at liberty to arrive at their own conclusions. My intention is to provide information for consideration.

I consider it a challenge to thumb through Scripture and draw attention to various parables, episodes and verses that are contained in the Bible, and then write about that material by commenting and asking questions. Asking questions is the most basic means of communicating with other people and it was what Jesus desired from those whom he taught. Many questions that I ask I have no idea as to the answer, but the questions are asked to provoke thought and create discussion. One can only imagine where thoughts may lead, and that, to me, is exciting!

I would like to emphasize an important expression that I have written below and also written again later in this book. Albert Einstein is considered by many as a highly intelligent and knowledgeable person in the field of physics and mathematics; in fact, when he discovered the theory of relativity $E = MC^2$, he was declared a genius, and rightly so! For me, though, I delight not in his scientific equation, but in his simple statement:

Imagination is better than knowledge!

Do You Fear the Wind?

by Hamlin Garland

Do you fear the force of the wind,
The slash of the rain?
Go face them and fight them,
Be savage again.
Go hungry and cold like the wolf,
Go wade like the crane:
The palms of your hands will thicken,
The skin of your cheek will tan,
You'll grow ragged and weary and swarthy,
But you'll walk like a man!

Robert W. Parrott

Dedication

I met Bob Parrott in the early 1970's, at which time he was in his early 60's. It was summer when he, his wife Leone and their daughter Jean visited our family farm. Our common interest was livestock, and in particular Shorthorn/Polled Shorthorn cattle. I vividly recall meeting them in what is still our present_day kitchen, and when I shook hands with him, I knew somehow there was an immediate connection. With hardly saying a word, I knew I needed to know him better.

Bob and my father Paul were practically the same age, so they had experienced many similar things in their lives while growing up, the main thing being the Depression. Bob, however, had spent some years serving his country during the war, whereas my father did not. My dad told me once though in later years that he regretted not having done so. Dad never did get too far from home and the house in which he was born for any length of time, the exceptions being a flight to family roots in Sweden, and vacations and sight_seeing in most parts of America. Dad lived in the same house for over 65 years, and then he and Mom moved to town. It was then that the Author of this book and his new bride occupied the home house. Hard to believe that this year 2006, I have lived in that same house 65 years also. The same kitchen table where I met Bob Parrott and his family is the same kitchen table where I asked my wife Carol to marry me.

At our first meeting I realized Bob Parrott had skills that few men possess. Were there rough edges? You bet! Was there a confidant assurance? Yes, there was! Was there a loving gentleness lying just below the surface? Absolutely! I grew to appreciate and respect those characteristics in the short time I had the opportunity to be around him. It was at a later time that the connection between us would become evident as we were both military veterans – WW II for Bob and Vietnam for me. I never did ask much about his experiences in the war; I just mainly listened.

Bob loved his family and the out_of_doors life of a cattleman, complete with buffalo grass and the ranch at Trails End. His education of being a college graduate complimented his ability to talk with people, and what I learned from him I try to pass on to the next generation. His passion for music was evident to me as country singer Eddy Arnold was a favorite. Bob likewise knew a good poet when he read one, and Badger Clark was the one. I still have in my possession the copy of Sun and Saddle Leather by Badger Clark that Bob sent me as a gift. I really appreciated him doing that and I still read it from time to time. My favorite poem, "The Free Wind," is written on the next page. Other favorite poems in the book are "Ridin'," and "The Old Cow Man." Both poems say something about Bob and my father. I miss them both a lot. My father was born in 1909 and passed away in 1982. Bob was born in 1908 and passed away in 1997. I would like to have known each of them much longer.

And so, this book is dedicated to Robert W. Parrott, friend of many, friend of mine, with special mention of his wife Leone and daughter Jean.

The Free Wind

by Badger Clark

I went and worked in a drippin' mine
 'Mong the rock and the oozin' wood,
For the dark seemed lit with a dollar sign
 And they told me money's good.
So I jumped and sweat for a flat_foot boss
 Till my pocket bulged with pay,
But my heart it fought like a led bronc hawse
 Till I flung my drill away.

For the wind, the wind, the good free wind,
 She sang from the pine divide
That the sky was blue and the young years few
 And the world was big and wide!
From the poor, bare hills all gashed with scars
 I rode till the range was crossed;
Then I watched the gold of sunset bars
And my camp_sparks glintin' toward the stars
 And laughed at the pay I'd lost.

I went and walked in the city way
 Down a glitterin' canyon street,
For the thousand lights looked good and gay
 And they said life there was sweet.
So the wimmen laughed while the night reeled by
 And the wine ran red and gold,
But their laugh was the starved wolf's huntin' cry
 And their eyes were hard and old.

And the wind, the wind, the clean free wind,
 She laughed through the April rains:
"Come out and live by the wine I give
 In the smell of the greenin' plains!"
And I looked back once to the smoky towers
 Where my face had bleached so pale,

Then I loped through the lash of drivin' showers
To the uncut sod and the prairie flowers
   And the old wide life o' the trail.

I went and camped in the valley trees
   Where the thick leaves whispered rest,
For love lived there 'mong the honey bees,
   And they told me love was best.
There the twilight lanes were cool and dim
   And the orchards pink with May,
Yet my eyes they'd lift to the valley's rim
   Where the desert reached away.

And the wind, the wind, the wild free wind,
   She called from the web love spun
To the unbought sand of the lone trail land
   And the sweet hot kiss o' the sun!
Oh, I looked back twice to the valley lass,
Then I set my spurs and sung,
For the sun sailed up above the pass
And the mornin' wind was in the grass
   And my hawse and me was young.

"After forty, not so good!"
Robert W. Parrott

Sun and Saddle Leather by Badger Clark

Acknowledgment and Thanks

Once again I want to thank Christine Dokolasa for her artistic work. As in the past, she has demonstrated the ability to produce fantastic sketches and art work. I appreciate her willingness to be part of my book. Thank you, Christine!

Also, I owe many thanks to Lori and Bob Reed of Reed Studios who have arranged the graphic lettering. Their expertise enhances the visual appearance and the quality of the sketches in my book. Thank you, Lori and Bob!

Lastly, I would never have completed this book without the assistance of my wife, Carol. For her part, many were the hours of reading through and critiquing the material presented. For all of her time and effort I truly appreciate everything she does to bring this book to completion. Thank you very much, Carol!

The Wind

The wind blows where it pleases.
You hear its sound, but you cannot tell where it comes from or where it is going.
So it is with everyone born of the Spirit.
John 3:8

With those words Jesus explained to Nicodemus what constitutes a person being "born again." This was something that should have been understood by Nicodemus because, after all, he was a learned religious scholar with impeccable credentials; he was of the elite class of the Pharisees, a member of the Jewish ruling council. Having said that, in Jesus' eyes Nicodemus knew next to nothing; in fact, he was nearly ignorant of important issues pertaining to God. He had studied scripture and he was accepted as one having great intellect, but somewhere along the line misconceptions had led him astray, and Jesus told him so!

To reveal to Nicodemus that being "born again" was not a process that a person completes, Jesus used the analogy of the wind. The characteristics of the wind according to verse eight are: 1) It goes where it wants to go; 2) You know it's there; and 3) You can't control it. Being "born again" and "born of the Spirit" have the wind in common. The wind is a phenomenon of nature that the ear can hear but the eye cannot see, no matter how hard a person may try. The wind is a force that can toss waves around in the sea as well as bend tree limbs closer to the ground. A strong north wind can make cold temperatures even colder, and wind from the south can make temperatures rise. Where is the wind's origin? No one knows! Where is the wind going? No one knows!

The Spirit has the same qualities as the wind according to this passage in John chapter 3. Is there any limit to its abilities? What is the Spirit's purpose? According to **John 16:13, "But when he, the Spirit of truth comes, he will guide you into all truth. He will not speak on his own; he will speak only what he hears, and he will tell you what is yet to come. He will bring glory to me by taking from what is mine and making it known to you. All that belongs to the Father is mine. That is why I said the Spirit will take from what is mine and make it known to you."**

So it is. The Spirit goes where it wants to go; you know it's there; and you can't control it! This agency has unlimited capabilities, and if a person will but listen to its sounds, the Spirit of truth will reveal information about God that makes sense.

Table of Contents

Note:

All quoted Bible verses are taken from
the New International Version (NIV),
unless otherwise noted.

The Author has purposely used lower case letters
in reference to God, Jesus, and the Holy Spirit.
For example, the words "he, him, his" that are used as
nouns, pronouns, or adjectives are not capitalized in this book.
This is done solely as the Author's preference.

Front and Back Covers _ Christine Dokolasa
Graphics _ Lori & Bob Reed, Reed Studios

Just Between You, Me,
and the Fence Post

By
Roger Setterdahl

"We live by faith,
not by sight."

2 Corinthians 5:7

The Children

"From the lips of children and infants you have ordained praise."
Psalm 8:2

<u>Language of a little child:</u>
"Daddy, doesn't God love us as much as Jesus does?"

<u>And you the parent ask:</u>
"How could you raise that question? How could you ask that?"

<u>The child replies:</u>
"Well, Jesus is pleading with God to forgive me for the things I did wrong today, so I know who's on my side!"

At a tender age, children acquire a sense of knowledge that surprises us older adults. Though their appearance may be naïve and uneducated, statements and episodes like the one quoted above bring the parent generations to their knees in awe. How can a child of so few years of age arrive at a summary of religious thought like that?

What has transpired in the teachings of Christianity for children to sense that God is a person to fear, that he's not a very friendly God? Oh, everyone knows how kind and gentle Jesus is, and how he is our friend who has shed his blood so the Father will accept us and forgive us. The younger generation has always known how nice Jesus is and how he wants children to climb upon his lap so he can put his arms around them. Youngsters know that Jesus is always smiling and that he has a wonderful disposition, that he is the embodiment of love, that he will always be there when needed, that he wants to be part of your life, that he would never do anything to harm anyone.

But look out for God! He is watching every move you make, and when you mess up just a little bit, he writes it down in his little black book where a permanent record is kept. Every time you do something wrong you can expect some kind of retribution because God's justice requires him to take the necessary steps to make sure it doesn't happen again. When it does though, God will discipline you, but it's for your own good! When anything worse does happen again by chance, you can always count on Jesus to make things right with God by accepting the punishment you deserve. Jesus will even die because he loves you so much!

With this kind of attitude it comes to the point where people are more afraid of God than they are of Satan, the devil. With Jesus by their side, he over_rules anything Satan can do, and with Jesus by their side, they will never have to be afraid of God! It's such an unfavorable picture of God the Father to say that he is not as friendly or forgiving or understanding as Jesus, his Son. The relationship between Jesus and his Father was clearly outlined and demonstrated when Jesus said: "If you've seen me, you've seen the Father."

Always remember:

Satan, the devil, is the enemy!   **God is on our side!!**

Pleading With God

"In that day you will no longer ask me anything. I tell you the truth, my Father will give you whatever you ask in my name. Until now you have not asked for anything in my name. Ask and you will receive, and your joy will be complete.

Though I have been speaking figuratively, a time is coming when I will no longer use this kind of language but will tell you plainly about my Father. In that day you will ask in my name. I am not saying that I will ask the Father on your behalf. No, the Father himself loves you because you have loved me and have believed that I came from God. I came from the Father and entered the world; now I am leaving the world and going back to the Father."

John 16:23_28

Why do we picture Jesus pleading with the Father? Why is it so hard to accept Jesus' own words in the Upper Room as being true? Previously, Jesus had just told the disciples that he wanted to treat them as friends:

"I no longer call you servants, because a servant does not know his master's business. Instead, I have called you friends, for everything that I learned from my Father I have made known to you."

John 15:15

And so, as friends (and not just as servants who do what they are told to do) the disciples are about to receive some clarification in regard to Jesus' role as mediator. In the past, it was thought that Jesus took our prayer requests to the Father and would plead our case before the throne, that he would even invoke his blood to appease the Father. These important words that Jesus expresses at this time that are recorded by John are absent in the other three gospels. It's wonderful that John has included them in his message because it sheds light on what God really wants. This is the climax of Jesus teaching the disciples and us about our relationship with him and his Father, and the relationship that has always existed between Jesus and his Father.

"I am not saying that I will ask the Father on your behalf." Why is that so? Because **"the Father himself loves you!"** What has Jesus just communicated to the disciples? He told them **"the Father himself loves you"** just as much as Jesus loves you; he always has in the past and he always will in the future. **God is love (1 John 4:16).** God has always been that way since day one, but Satan, the devil, has woven his deceptive picture of God into the people's belief system, and the people bought into his misrepresentation and lies about God. What Jesus is saying in this passage is important because there has always been an open line of communication available between God and human beings. From God's perspective, a mediator or a 'go_between' was never needed or necessary, but when people became influenced by the devil's tactics and became afraid of God, there was little God could do but provide someone to act as the mediator. It was Moses who was chosen to represent the people to God and vice_versa. And from all of that sprang the ceremonial system of sacrifices and relying on someone else to talk to God instead of doing it yourself.

It has always been God's desire for personal relationships, with no mediator and no one 'in_between.' As far back as Moses, the people were either afraid or disinterested in having first_hand contact with God, so God reluctantly gave them the priestly mediator who would intercede for them. It wasn't what he wanted, but at least there would be some kind of communication between God and his people.

Few realized it, but with Jesus' presence in their midst there was actually no mediator between them and God because Jesus was God. Think about how comfortable many individuals were when around Jesus. That is exactly how people are to be around the Father _ the same identical way! But when Jesus revealed that he was God, the religious community rejected him because they had a different picture of what God should be like. God surely couldn't be One they could see and touch with their own hands. Jesus encouraged them, if nothing else, to **"believe the miracles, that you may know and understand that the Father is in me, and I in the Father." John 10:38.** It is so unfortunate that during Jesus' three years of ministry **"they did not understand that he was telling them about his Father." John 8:27.**

The constant looking at self is the devil's deception because looking at self takes a person's focus off of God. If we as people cannot see beyond our own imperfections and see God instead, we likewise **"do not understand."** We need to see God as he truly is and quit feeling sorry for our pitiful condition of begging and imploring God to forgive us. We need to get past the 'feel_sorry_for_self' syndrome and the constant attitudes that "I need Jesus blood; I'm not good enough." Folks, none of us are good enough! We need to be **"transformed by the renewing of our minds." Rom. 12:2.** We need to be willing to **"put on the new self, which is being renewed in knowledge in the image of its Creator." Col. 3:10.** We need to be learn from God as Jesus said: **"They will all be taught by God. Everyone who listens to the Father and learns from him comes to me." John 6:45.**

If Jesus had not come to reveal his Father, we may not have known how to approach him. We would probably have remained afraid of him, never knowing for sure what to do, when to do it, or how to do it! We may even have thought that we needed to bring all kinds of offerings and gifts to win his attention. Picture the meeting of Jesus and the disciples in the Upper Room just prior to Gethsemane and the Cross. The disciples did nothing to win Jesus' attention; in fact, they didn't even wash Jesus' feet before supper. What were they thinking about? Notice that Jesus did not berate them. So what happened? Jesus just sat down to supper with dirty feet! (see John 13:1_17).

We need to remind ourselves of what Jesus said: **"Anyone who has seen me has seen the Father." John 14:9.** If the Father would have come instead of Jesus, he would have sat down to supper with dirty feet also, and he wouldn't have been offended by it. We all make mistakes, and Jesus and the Father know that, but they still love us unconditionally anyway. Forgiveness is not a problem with them. When Jesus uttered those words of forgiveness on the Cross, it didn't mean that everyone would be saved. It meant that his attitude toward us has always been and will always be one of forgiveness. It will remain that way forever, and even when people are dying the second death, Jesus will not look at them and say: "Justice is being served because I am not only loving _ I am just!" God is not a two_sided God. He is always loving and righteous and forgiving, and he tearfully watches his sinful children perish in spite of all of his efforts. **God does not forgive on the one hand and seek eternal punishment on the other.**

I do not picture God looking upon the lost with a sense of supreme justice and satisfaction that they are getting the deserved punishment for the crime committed. I believe at that time there will be a scene of extreme sadness, especially on God's part because there will be no future resurrection for the lost. For those that are lost, tomorrow will not exist. There may be some who are insecure with a God who seems so kind and forgiving, one who would unashamedly cry over those not in his kingdom, but if God is not truly lamenting over his lost angels and human beings created in his image, then those who inhabit the courts in Heaven may never be sure they can trust him.

Jesus didn't come to tell us how bad we are.
He came to tell us how good God is!

The Wooden End Post

["If Fence Posts Could Speak"]

As is most cases, the last fence post to rot and deteriorate, and finally fall to the ground is *the end post*, _ more specifically known as *the anchor post*. This post may also be referred to as *the corner post*, especially if it is located in the corner of a field. Primarily due to its size, its prominence, and its location sometimes as a boundary marker between lands of separate ownership, *the end post* is usually "*the last man standing*."

Where land acreage no longer has need for fence and barbed wire, this lonely post serves as the sentinel who proudly reigns over his private corner of the world. He is impressive, especially since nearly all of his comrades have either fallen by the wayside as victims of old age, or they have been intentionally removed and disposed of in a proper manner, a demeaning finality to unneeded tradition and purpose. Alone, and in his position of dominance, *the end post* is the sole remaining reminder of what has been. He is the record of history that has accurately and triumphantly recorded all of the activity in his neighborhood. He has stored within himself all of the vital information and knowledge concerning his entire life, and it is up to us to retrieve that information and learn from it. We need to know his roots, but in reality it does little good to converse directly with *the end post*. Our objective and what is required of us is that we would be willing to listen to his words of knowledge and wisdom, because there is much that he can say about his life and his experiences, and there is much that we can learn from him if we are willing to spend the time doing so. Because *the end post* is sturdy as well as stubborn, we would do well to show respect and even admiration for him, all the while realizing and visualizing where he came from. After all, *the wooden end post* was once a tree.

The Prodigal Son

[Luke 15:11_32]

Trudging hesitantly on the dirt path toward home and not knowing quite sure what to expect, the Prodigal Son finally ascends the crest of the hill, and there in full view is the home he left for good not long ago. Looking intently from afar, the Son can see that at the corner of the pathway that leads to his father's home is that familiar old End Post, still standing in the same place as when he left. There are tears in his eyes as the Prodigal Son seeks some inner strength, but thoughts of disappointment from his father are becoming unbearable. He wonders to himself: Will his father accept him back? Will his father want him back? Will his father forgive him?

The Son's emotions become so over_powering that he decides to rest for a moment on the road bank and gather his thoughts. So, sitting alone in the roadside ditch with his face buried in his hands, his eyes closed, and his head resting on his knees, the Prodigal Son is contemplating what might happen next. "You need to get your act together," he says while talking to himself. "You need to plan how you're going to respond to your father." The Prodigal Son is oblivious to anything else that is happening around him.

Little does the Prodigal Son know what has transpired the moment he sat down along the roadside ditch, because that familiar old End Post at the corner of the pathway was not alone _ it had a visitor. It was at the End Post that the father had made his daily trek and vigil. It was there that the father would sometimes place his fingers on top of the post with his head bent down looking at the ground, where he would sometimes lean with his back against the post, all the while waiting and watching for his Son to come home. Can you picture the father there, day after day, yearning to catch a glimpse of his wayward Son, hoping that each day would be the day that his Son would return? Pouring out his heart to the End Post, the father exposed his inner thoughts and his heart's desires. The father knows, though, that the End Post is nothing more than just a post, but that doesn't mean his inner_most thoughts went unheard. Someone was listening!

Today, as the father was again leaning with his back against the End Post, his eyes gazed down the road once more, and from a long distance away he recognized his Son, plodding along the road, but now resting along the road bank, pondering his fate and his next move. Quickly the father abandons his position at the End Post and runs as he has never run before toward his Son, shouting loudly to himself: "He's back! He's back! My Son is back! My Son has come home!"

Question: What was the son's problem?

Answer: _____.

Question: When was the son forgiven by his father?

Answer: _____.

The Prodigal Son

Part One:
Running Away From Home.

Question: What was the son's problem?
   Answer: He wanted to live his life without any restraints.

The Problem.

It was obvious. The younger son knew absolutely that his father favored the older son, as it was he who was entrusted with the management of the family farm. Not that the younger son wasn't "learning the ropes" as he grew in maturity, it's just that the difference in age was a definite factor. Experience, due to age, separated the two brothers. Also, the older son accepted the position of being in charge of their father's estate, and was very dedicated to his father.

The younger son faced the reality that his older brother would most likely carry on the tradition of their father, and he realized that no matter how hard he tried, his efforts would always fall short of those of older brother. It all became clearer with the passage of time that the compatibility of younger and older brother was in jeopardy. Knowing full well the custom of generational inheritance, the younger son opts out early in life. He decides it's time for him to split _ take the money and run!

Can you picture the younger son there as he accepts his share of his father's inheritance? Is there a tear in his eye? Is he weeping inside? Perhaps he is a bit vocal with a somewhat harsh tone of voice. Whatever may be the case, the younger leaves abruptly for the big city in that distant country where he quickly and foolishly manages to squander his entire inheritance. One moment he possesses his entire fortune; the next moment _ next to nothing! At that moment it didn't matter to the younger because he was living his life without any restraints. He was a free man!

Question: When was the son forgiven by his father?
   Answer: After he returned home, and confessed and apologized to his father.

The Forgiveness.

It was obvious. Living in the pig pen was no bed of roses. Hungry, filthy, in need of life's basics, the younger "came to his senses." (vs. 17). He was still rational in his mind as he realistically figured out his true position when he blew it all. Life in the big city swallowed up every meaningful thought he had learned on the farm in the presence of his father and older brother. Plenty of warning signs were there, but the younger chose to disregard them and live his life as he thought best.

But now, having come to his senses while in the pig pen, the younger knew life for him would be much better if he were to return home and become his father's hired man. Living conditions at home were positively better than facing starvation with the pigs. The younger was desperate. Life in the big city did not turn out like he had dreamt it would. Admitting to himself that he had lost his inheritance, that he had spent time with prostitutes, the younger sees home on the farm as a pretty good place after all. The younger decides to return home.

But wait! Now that he came to his senses, he knew what he must do. He needs to apologize to his father, and hopefully his father will accept him and forgive him, and allow him to be part of the family again. If necessary, the younger will beg forgiveness so he can be restored to fellowship in the family that he once deserted. The younger will even become the least of all servants in his father's household, the lowest of all slaves. The younger wants only to return home.

With his apology speech memorized and with deep sorrow and conviction, the younger confesses to his father: "Father, I have sinned against heaven and against you. I am no longer worthy to be called your son." (vs. 18, 19). So, with this statement of confession, the father forgives his wayward son for squandering his entire inheritance, and reconciliation within the family takes place. Father and son fellowship is restored.

The Prodigal Son

Part Two:
Failure to understand his father.

Question: What was the son's problem?
    Answer: He had the wrong picture of his father.

The Problem.

It wasn't so obvious. It didn't matter that the younger son (as well as the older son) had grown from infancy under the watchful and loving eye of their father. However, it did matter that their father would establish a unique relationship with each of his sons, and that those relationships would be nurtured, cared for, and protected from harmful influence. Even with only two sons to be responsible for, surely there would be adequate time and effort to devote to each son. Surely the father would do the right thing.

As human beings, one can only imagine the thoughts that go through the mind of another person, and even though that person is dear to the heart and even the closest of a close family member or friend, crawling into someone else's thought process is no easy chore. It's highly probable the attempt to do so is futile, and any conclusions reached are at best pure guess_work, even though learned scholars who are considered experts in that field may disagree.

Close family relationships just don't naturally happen, and many are the times when the best efforts on everyone's part are put forth, and yet the outcome is not congenial. Friction develops and after only so long, there becomes a parting of the way. And when family estates are involved, there almost always is some sort of prearranged settlement. It appears this was the case with the Prodigal Son.

The younger son: requested his share of his father's inheritance; left home for the bright lights of the big city; lost his entire allotment on foolish indulgence; ended up in the pig pen hungry, dirty and broke. But the younger did come to his senses (vs. 17), and he realized he would be better off back home on the farm under his father's guidance, even as a servant. Forget about being a son to his father! The younger yearned for what he thought he had lost.

The younger son's real problem was that he had the wrong picture of his father. He didn't realize beforehand how much his father loved him, that he was important to his father. It wasn't until he heard it himself from his father's lips that the younger knew in his heart that his father's attitude toward him was overflowing with love and concern. Regardless of what he had done in the past, or what he would do in the future, the younger would always be considered the father's pride and joy. The younger son's episode in the big city was a learning experience that demonstrated what can happen in the course of life and in the boundaries of family relationships.

Question: When was the son forgiven by the father?
  Answer: Before he left home to go on his journey.

The Forgiveness.

It wasn't so obvious. Family relationships are the ones that are most important to sincere and loving people. If family members are experiencing stress and trials that add strain and tension to personal relationships, something needs to be in place within the framework of the family circle that will be beneficial and offer a remedy that will provide needed relief. True forgiveness would undoubtedly be the answer.

Everyone makes mistakes. It may appear that some people make more than their share of mistakes, but the final analysis may prove otherwise. I would estimate it would all even out in the end. Failure in one person's eyes may be a winner in someone else's eyes. Sometimes it appears that the victory goes to a particular person, but yet, it may not actually be that way. That particular victory could be fleeting. To the victor go the spoils? Perhaps!

The younger son experienced defeat when he left home _ he came in (nearly) dead last! There wasn't anything to be proud of as his achievements were certainly not worth 'writing home about.' His reputation as a loser was well known and established in the whole neighborhood as his older brother testified upon his arrival back home (vs. 30). But none of this concerned the younger son's father in the least! All that the father wanted was for his son to come home. It didn't matter that the inheritance was wasted in its entirety! So what if there was nothing left! What mattered was that the family relationship would be restored, and there was fellowship once again. Nothing, absolutely nothing, else mattered.

The father had been looking for the younger son's return for some time. What joy must have filled his heart when the reunion of his family commenced. The father wanted to hear nothing of his son's repentance because there was no need for it. The father had established that fact within the boundaries of the family relationship before any act of separation could occur. The father forgave the son before he left home. Nothing, absolutely nothing, would interfere by any act of any family member with forgiveness. The son found this to be true as the father embraced him and called for a celebration. The younger son "was dead but is alive again; he was lost and is found." (vs. 32). What a joyous occasion!

Most of us are like the Prodigal Son:
  We take our due inheritance and run,
  and we likewise quickly and totally squander every ounce of it.

  Are we failures? _ no doubt!
  Are we wasteful? _ yes, indeed!
  Are we able to "come to our senses?" Absolutely!

Do we realize and know that God forgives us <u>before</u> we individually go on our journey of life? It's easy for God to forgive because **God is Forgiveness Personified!** That is the way God is! It's just that if we don't know that about him, we might not leave the pig pen,...and come home to a waiting Father. It's inevitable we will make mistakes, that "we have sinned against our Father in heaven and are no longer worthy to be called his son" (vs. 21). Our Father counters that with: "Listen! I am forgiveness personified! I forgave you from time immortal! In my family, forgiveness is priority #1! I am a healing God who wants you and everyone else to know and understand what I am all about! I am a God who desires your respect and companionship, and I am a God who delights in your freedom. I want us to be friends! I want you to be part of my family, part of my eternal neighborhood! You have the right to accept me and the right to reject me, _ that decision is yours to make. I only ask that I be given the opportunity to present evidence about myself!"

Could it be stated that:
True Friendship is Total Forgiveness?

What prevents us from totally forgiving someone else?

<u>**How to escape from the pig pen:**</u>   <u>**Change your view of God!**</u>

God wants to treat you as a loyal son, not as a hired servant or a slave.
God is constantly looking down the road for your return home.

<u>**The main thing is: Be sure you come home!**</u>
Nothing else matters to God!

The "If's"

The Wilderness of Temptation.

[Matthew 4:1_11; Luke 4:1_13].

1. The tempter came to him and said,
    "<u>If</u> you are the Son of God, tell these stones to become bread."

    Matt. 4:3

Undoubtedly, Jesus was physically hungry. Could Jesus have changed the stones into bread? Absolutely! Could Satan the devil have done this also? Yes, he could have! Why did Jesus refuse to do it? Did he refuse because to do so would not have been reliable and believable evidence? Jesus answered,

> **"It is written: 'Man shall not live on bread alone, but on every word that comes from the mouth of God'." (see Deut. 8:3)**
>
> **Matt. 4:4**

2. Then the devil took him to the holy city and had him stand on the highest point of the temple. "**<u>If</u> you are the Son of God**," he said, "**throw yourself down. For it is written: 'He will command his angels concerning you, and they will lift you up in their hands, so that you will not strike your foot against a stone'.**"
    (see Ps. 91:11, 12).

    Matt. 4:5, 6

What purpose did the devil, a created angel being, have in quoting this verse? Was he trying to have authority over the Son of God?

> Jesus answered him, **"It is also written: 'Do not put the Lord your God to the test'."**
> **(see Deut. 6:16).**
>
> **Matt. 4:7**

3. Again, the devil took him to a very high mountain and showed him all the kingdoms of the world and their splendor.

    "All this I will give you, he said, "<u>if</u> you will bow down and worship me."

    Matt. 4:9

Jesus said to him, **"Away from me, Satan! For it is written: 'Worship the Lord your God, and serve him only'." (see Deut. 6:13).**

Matt. 4:10

Then the devil left him, and angels came and attended him.

"If" is such a small prepositional word, but it has features that are not found in other words, namely that it is a highly conditional word. **"If** you do that, I will do this!" An action of one kind will be followed by action of another kind. In the case involving Jesus' Temptation, **"if"** is expressed to cause doubt in Jesus' mind, and at the same time **"if"** is expressed to accuse Jesus of being someone he was not. Satan conceived to work as much as he could to his advantage, but, of course, he failed. Satan was no match for the intelligence that Jesus possessed; neither was he a match for the truth that enveloped Jesus.

Deuteronomy 13

"If a prophet, or one who foretells by dreams, appears among you and announces to you a miraculous sign or wonder, and **if** the sign or wonder of which he has spoken takes place, and he says, 'Let us follow other gods,' (gods which you have not known) 'and let us worship them,' you must not listen to the words of that prophet or dreamer. The Lord your God is testing you to find out whether you love him with all your heart and with all your soul. It is the Lord your God you must follow, and him you must revere." (vs. 1_4).

"If your very own brother, or your son or daughter, or the wife you love, or your closest friend secretly entices you, saying, 'Let us go and worship other gods' (gods that neither you nor your fathers have known, gods of the peoples around you, whether near or far, from one end of the land to the other), do not yield to him or listen to him. Show him no pity. Do not spare him or shield him." (vs. 6_8).

"If you hear it said about one of the towns the Lord your God is giving you to live in that wicked men have arisen among you and have led the people of their town astray, saying, 'Let us go and worship other gods' (gods you have not known), then you must **inquire, probe, and investigate it thoroughly**. (vs. 12_14).

"And **if** it is true and it has been proved that this detestable thing has been done among you, you must certainly put to the sword all who live in that town. Destroy it completely, both its people and its livestock." (vs. 14, 15).

The events of the last book written by Moses occurred just prior to the entrance of God's people into the Promised Land. Sadly, the death of Moses is the last recorded entry in his book. As the "friend of God," Moses will always be revered as a great man who walked with God. Though called the Leader of the children of Israel, he was more importantly a Follower of God. In this thirteenth chapter of Deuteronomy, the words **"if"** have special significance because of the warnings attached to them. It's clear to Moses that **"if"** a particular action is taken, the pending result will be "this." More specifically, "**if** individuals go after other gods, the result will not be pleasant." In order to avoid the undesirable, Moses says, "do not listen to them in the first place! Avoid that which is wrong. Stay away from them!" Moses told the people to "look for the evidence" in order to determine right from wrong, and to do it until they were satisfied with the results of the investigation. Spare no amount of searching to find truth.

There would be no temptation to "follow other gods" if individuals initially had the correct picture of the only God. The urge to "try something new" was appealing, but in the setting of this period of time, it would become a disaster. Moses offered sound advice then to all who might possibly be led astray by following other gods. The same advice applies to us as well today.

Two Criminals - Two Crosses

[Luke 23:39_42]

Which criminal are you?   **Which cross are you on?**

"Aren't you the Christ?
Save yourself and us!"
                    (v. 39)

"Jesus, remember me when
you come into your kingdom."
                    (v. 42)

<u>Selfish Attitude and Claims:</u>

It's all about me, me, me!
My personal salvation is at stake!
<u>Claims of</u>: I don't deserve this!
I've been saved! I've been born again!
    I can read my own heart!

<u>Living, Trusting Relationship</u>:

It's all about God, not myself.
It's what God knows about me.
God knows me better than I know
        myself.
God alone can read my heart.

Two Criminals _ Two Crosses

[Luke 23:39_43]

One of the criminals who hung there hurled insults at him:
"Aren't you the Christ? Save yourself and us!"

But the other criminal rebuked him.
"Don't you fear God," he said, "since you are under the same sentence?
We are punished justly, for we are getting what we deserve.
But this man has done nothing wrong."

Then he said. "Jesus, remember me when you come into your kingdom."

Jesus answered him, "I tell you the truth today,
you will be with me in paradise."

Two criminals _ Two crosses

Which one are you?

Are you like the first criminal who:
1. Insults Jesus?
2. Pleads with Jesus?
3. Is concerned only with personal salvation?
4. Thinks only of 'me, me, me?'

or

Are you like the second criminal who:
1. Rebukes the first criminal for his incorrect assessment of Christ?
2. Realizes the truth about himself as well as the truth about Jesus?
3. Simply trusts Jesus and asks to be remembered?

The first criminal didn't like the way he was being treated so he berated Jesus for not being privy to his situation. He expected much from Jesus, but Jesus knew his heart and his real condition. This passage in Luke does not confirm any acknowledgment from Jesus to the first criminal as both hung on separate crosses. Did Jesus completely and purposely ignore him? Had the criminal passed 'the point of no return' in times past, and Jesus knew that? Had Jesus' patience been exhausted a long time before this episode, and he wasn't interested in any form of communication? Did the first criminal realize he was a self_centered individual and wanted Jesus only for selfish reasons, like saving him in his time of 'last_minute' need?

The second criminal was just as much a criminal as was the first one _ there was no denying that! Was he repentant? Did he confess all of his sins? Did he shed tears for a misused and wasted life that was about to end in an excruciating manner? Was he positive that Jesus would accept him? Did he even say "Thank you" to Jesus when he heard Jesus utter words of promise to him? What criteria did Jesus know about the second criminal that made him safe to save and become part of God's kingdom? The great thing about the second criminal was that he recognized God in this brief encounter, and that, in Jesus' eyes, made him safe to admit to the kingdom.

Could these two criminals be symbolic of the end_time judgment that will take place as the decision is made either for entering Heaven and New Jerusalem, or for being left outside the walls to suffer in the flames? Both criminals had equal opportunity during their lifetimes to become acquainted with Jesus, as they both called on his name. How would Jesus have looked upon the first criminal as he asked to be saved? Since Jesus did not respond to him verbally according to Luke, could their eyes have ever met, and if so, what kind of look would Jesus have had on his face? Would it have been a sly smirk that said "you're getting what you deserve; do you like it?" Could Jesus have been thinking to himself: "you should be suffering a lot worse than this for what you did?" Instead, would Jesus have shown sadness for the first criminal? Would Jesus have had a smile of satisfaction on his face when he heard the second criminal say what he said? Wouldn't that have been heart_warming to hear? Jesus didn't have much success that day, but he did win one person _ the second criminal caught a glimpse of God while looking at Jesus. That was all the evidence he needed to become one of Jesus' followers.

This episode and conversation recorded by Luke is not found in any of the other gospels. I wonder why! Why did Luke insert it in his account when the others did not, especially taking into account that it was the disciple John who is mentioned as being acknowledged by Jesus while on the Cross.

Listening

"The Man Born Blind"

A second time they summoned the man who had been born blind.
"Give glory to God," they said.
"We know this man (Jesus) is a sinner."
He replied, "Whether he is a sinner or not, I don't know.
One thing I do know. I was blind but now I see!"
Then they asked him,
"What did he do to you? How did he open your eyes?"
He answered:
"I have told you already and you did not listen.
Why do you want to hear it again?
Do you want to become his disciples, too?"

Then they hurled insults at him and said:
"You are this fellow's disciple! We are disciples of Moses.
We know that God spoke to Moses, but as for this fellow,
we don't even know where he comes from."

The man answered, "Now that is remarkable!
You don't know where he comes from, yet he opened my eyes.
We know that God does not listen to sinners.
He listens to the godly man who does his will.
Nobody has ever heard of opening the eyes of a man born blind.
If this man were not from God, he could do nothing."

To this they replied,
"You were steeped in sin at birth; how dare you lecture us!"
And they threw him out.

John 9:24_34

No One Is Listening

The importance of learning how to listen cannot be over_emphasized. It takes training and practice, practice, practice to listen well because it is so easy to "tune out" that which you do not want to hear, or take the time to hear. Imagine for a moment being the blind man and never having been able to "see" anything your entire life until one day a man named Jesus restored that which had never been done before: complete vision. How would you react to this miracle? What would be your testimony?

John 9:1_41.

The entire chapter of John 9 describes the story of The Man Born Blind. It is a wonderful setting for Jesus to demonstrate who the blind really are. It turns out those who condemned the man born blind and his parents also, were the ones who couldn't see, that they didn't understand much about anything except they thought they knew everything about everything! Not only could they not "see," they were very poor listeners also. Because they "knew" everything, they didn't need to listen to anyone, especially a person who was born blind. How could he know anything when he lacked vision to read? The blind man's perception with his ears must have been astounding. Even modern_day blind people seem to have a sixth sense or awareness that non_blind people have not.

"You are a king, then!" said Pilate.
Jesus answered, "You are right in saying I am a king.
In fact, for this reason I was born, and for this I came into the world, to testify to the truth.
<u>Everyone on the side of truth listens to me."</u>

John 18:37

Obedience _ a willingness to listen and learn.

During Jesus' ministry of three and a half years, the ability to listen by those to whom he spoke was a problem, just as it is today. Resistance to taking adequate time to understand someone else usually has impatience and reluctance to deal with too. It's always easier to end the conversation abruptly with a short brief statement, or a person can express body language that demonstrates the same thing. Even in the verse quoted above concerning Pilate, there was little effort made on his part to listen to Jesus' reply to his question "What is truth?" I often wonder what Jesus would have said to him and what John would have recorded if Pilate would have stayed to listen. One can only surmise it would have been answered in an easy_to_understand way.

Peter, at Solomon's Colonnade.

Peter was speaking boldly and to the point while addressing a group of people gathered at the place called Solomon's Colonnade. It was at this time and place that Peter reminded and declared for all to hear who was responsible for Jesus' death. Make no mistake about it _ insane religious people killed God! What Peter said to them must have rung in their ears as they listened to him say:

**"The God of Abraham, Isaac and Jacob, the God of our fathers,
has glorified his servant Jesus. You handed him over to be killed,
and you disowned him before Pilate, though he had decided to let him go.
You disowned the Holy and Righteous One and asked that a murderer be released to you.
You killed the Author of Life, but God raised him from the dead.**

Acts 3:13_15

It would have been easy to ignore what Peter said to this group of people and then leave the premises. Peter realized that having said what he did to them, there was still reason for them to stick around and listen some more because even though the blame for Christ's death was made clear to them, there was hope if they would listen to Peter say:

**"Now, brothers, I know you acted in ignorance, as did your leaders.
But this is how God fulfilled what he had foretold through all the prophets,
saying that his Christ would suffer. Repent, then, and turn to God,
so that your sins may be wiped out, that time of refreshing may come from the Lord,
and that he may send the Christ, who has been appointed for you _ even Jesus.
He must remain in heaven until the time comes for God to restore everything,
as he promised long ago through his holy prophets.
For Moses said, "The Lord your God will raise up for you a prophet like me
from among your own people; you must listen to everything he tells you.
Anyone who does not listen to him will be completely cut off from among his people.**

Acts 3:17_23

The Transfiguration.

**After six days Jesus took with him Peter, James and John the brother of James,
and led them up a high mountain by themselves.
There he was transfigured before them. His face shone like the sun,
and his clothes became as white as the light.
Just then there appeared before them Moses and Elijah, talking with Jesus.**

Peter said to Jesus, "Lord, it is good for us to be here. If you wish,
I will put up three shelters _ one for you, one for Moses and one for Elijah."
While he was still speaking, a bright cloud enveloped them,
And a voice from the cloud said,
"This is my Son, whom I love; with him I am well pleased.
<u>Listen to him!</u>"

Matt. 17:1_5

May we all learn how to listen to God.

Before It Happens

[John 13:19; 14:29]

<u>Question</u>: **Would evil have come into existence if Lucifer, the archangel who became Satan the devil, had been satisfied with God being the only Creator?**

God knows best in all situations. He alone can be trusted with creative powers, and even though it can be thought that we as human beings would always consult God in matters of great importance, God knows our inner_most thoughts and the real reasons for our actions and decisions.

It all started before creation of planet Earth thousands of years ago. In the spaces of Heaven, it was Lucifer, the archangel, who decided that he deserved the same creative powers as that of his Creator, God. His beauty and pride thrust him to the forefront of the entire composite of created angels, and it seemed so natural that he should be entitled to the same amount of power as God. After all, he was the most articulate and beautiful and most important angel that inhabited the courts of Heaven. (Lucifer's characteristics are found in Ezekiel 28:12_19 where it records God's lament against the king of Tyre, a type of the angel Lucifer. Additional information about Lucifer is found in Isaiah 14:12_14). Regardless, Lucifer had a major flaw _ he was jealous of God. On top of that it was clear to God that Lucifer lacked the ability to realize what the fatal outcome would be if creative powers were given to him. For Lucifer, all that mattered to him was that he be endowed with this authority, and even by vowing to use his new capabilities in a manner consistent with that of God's, our heavenly Father could do nothing less than to deny Lucifer that power and authority.

Sadly, Lucifer didn't understand. God's decision not to allow anyone else to possess creative powers brought the rebel attitude to the surface of Lucifer's mind, and it was then but a short step to accusations and open rebellion against his Creator. It was painful for an important angel of Lucifer's stature to be left out of the creative process, as in his mind he had the same capabilities as that of God. But God knew better! God knew that even an angel of Lucifer's willingness to do good things could not be fully trusted, and it would not be safe to allow him or other created angels the ability to create.

God did not leave Lucifer and the other angels with an open and shut case, nor did he say that they would have to just trust his judgment on this. God intended to prove his ability to do right. What God did must have astounded the entire Universe of angels at that time, because this was no consortium of a God who would implement a plan and take anyone by surprise. What God did was to start in motion the creation of planet Earth, with plants and animals, and finally with people who were created in the image of God, and that image included **the ability to think, to make choices, to know God, and to act.** These people were also given the ability to pro_create which was the closest act that God could do in giving the ability to create. Since God in his wisdom did not give angels the power to create nor the power to pro_create, the events of the entire creation of the planet we live on is God's answer to Lucifer's implication that he deserved the same creative powers as that of God. Planet Earth is God's ongoing demonstration that he knows beforehand the result of giving creative authority and power to those whom he has created, angels as well as men.

While Lucifer and all of the other created angels were denied creative powers as well as the ability to pro_create (to reproduce in their own image), God was willing to demonstrate that his decision was correct: **Better to leave all creative powers to God.** This was a nightmare to Lucifer and his followers, and was totally unacceptable. They could not comprehend God's reluctance to limit himself to this kind of power and authority. For us as humans, we can but look at the full picture of Earth's history and nod our approval: God did the right thing for sure! Look at the mess pro_creation has gotten itself into since this planet became our home. It is not a very pretty picture! Like Jesus states in the gospel of John:

> **"I have told you now before it happens,**
> **so that when it does happen, you will believe."**
>
> **John 14:29**

Folks, it happened just the way God said it would happen.

If pro_creation is the closest resemblance to creation that is possible, then we, the human race, are the primary participants in this demonstration. The animal kingdom, as well as the plant kingdom that humans depend on for physical life, are also examples of pro_creation as they, too, have the same capability of reproduction. For the human race, the unification of a tiny sperm and an egg completes the process that we know and experience as pro_creation. "Be fruitful and multiply" was endowed to everything that God created in regard to planet Earth. How utterly different this was when compared to the created angels that took place long before this earthly creation took place. All of the angels (loyal angels as well the rebellious) needed to understand without question the outcome if God was to give them creative power. The human race provides that convincing evidence.

It was not without trepidation and foreknowledge that God initiated his demonstration over a lengthy span of time, even thousands of years, although it can be seen from the record that almost immediately God's decision to limit creative powers was correct. What happened almost immediately in the Garden of Eden? God initially made Adam out of the dust of the earth; he breathed into his lungs the breath of life, and man became a living soul. God gave Adam power and dominion over the animals and the plants, but there was something still missing, as there was no means of continuing the human race with just one man. Man needed a helper, and God provided the necessary component to ensure the completion of evidence that the heavenly angels would need. The stage was set for the demonstration of pro_creation in the human race.

"Before It Happens."

Before <u>what</u> happens? What is it that Jesus tells us "before it happens?" Is this just another generalized prophetic statement? Is it important? <u>What</u> is going to happen? To <u>what</u> is Jesus referring?

John 13:18 20. Jesus Predicts His Betrayal.
"I am not referring to all of you; I know those I have chosen. But this is to fulfill the scripture: 'He who shares my bread has lifted up his heel against me.' **I am telling you now, so that when it does happen you will believe that I am He.** I tell you the truth, whoever accepts anyone I send accepts me; and whoever accepts me accepts the one who sent me."

John 14:28 31. Jesus Comforts His Disciples.
"You have heard me say, 'I am going away and I am coming back to you.' If you loved me, you would be glad that I am going to the Father, for the Father is greater than I. **I have told you now before it happens, so that when it does happen you will believe.** I will not speak with you much longer, for the prince of this world is coming. He has no hold on me, but the world must learn that I love the Father and that I do exactly what my Father has commanded me."

> <u>Mark 13:23</u> **is similar to John's recordings.**
> **"I have told you everything ahead of time."**

> <u>Amos 3:7</u> **is likewise of prophetic nature.**
> **"Surely the Sovereign Lord does nothing without revealing his plan to his servants the prophets."**

It appears from John's recording of two prophetic statements that Jesus is emphasizing two important points in his ministry. The first statement, (found in chapter 13), deals with Jesus' death. As always, Jesus "knows" everything beforehand. He "knows" Judas is the betrayer. He "knows" that the one who shares bread with the Creator of the Universe "has lifted up his heel against" him. Jesus is not surprised in the least! The second statement (found in chapter 14) concerns Jesus' return to Heaven and to his heavenly Father. As stated to his disciples, we should be glad Jesus is returning to Heaven because that means he has been accepted by his Father. Jesus came to do the demonstration of what God was like, and his Father declares that Jesus has exhibited the Father's nature completely and correctly.

Whether it was the angels who did not receive pro_creationism, or whether it was human beings who did receive pro_creationism, it makes no difference. God willingly provided the evidence that would convince everyone, especially Lucifer and the other rebellious angels, that to grant power to create outside of God would be a tragic mistake.

There are only minor opposing characteristics between angels and human beings. The angels are separate and unique entities; they can associate with each other; they can be evil in nature or they can be orderly and loving in nature. The number of angels cannot increase because they have no means of adding to their created number, unless God chooses to create more of them. Death of one angel means that their total number will be less than the original number that was created. In the case of angels, "evil" can only increase by intensity, not by the number of those possessing evil characteristics, and the same is true in like manner with the increase in "good." Good can only increase in intensity also.

The human aspect is similar in that human beings are separate and unique entities; they can associate with each other; and they can likewise be evil in nature or they can be good, orderly and loving in nature. As opposed to angels, human beings can increase in number because they possess the ability to pro_create. With that in mind, evil in this case can increase not only by intensity but also by number, and pro_creation accommodates this characteristic. The death of one human being does not necessarily mean a decrease in number as it does with angels because the birth rate of the human race far exceeds that of the death rate.

Creation and Pro Creation.

It doesn't matter. Each has the ability to love God; each has the ability to despise God. It's almost unbelievable, but it happened! The evil desire for power and control are easily transferred from Satan to those who agree with him and become like him. This is accomplished by instilling in the mind such thoughts as: "I am so good! I have been elected to fill this important position! I am the mediator between God and these poor illiterate people! I represent God and have the authority to forgive sins!" One thought builds upon another thought until the ultimate thought arrives: "Yes, I am just like God!" Concerning this attitude, the Apostle Paul clearly states:

"Don't let anyone deceive you in any way, for that day will not come until the rebellion occurs and the man of lawlessness is revealed, the man doomed to destruction. He will oppose and will exalt himself over everything that is called God or is worshiped, so that he sets himself up in God's temple, proclaiming himself to be God."

2 Thess. 2:3, 4

The inclinations of the carnal self_centered mind oppose the peace and security of the mind of God _ the two of them cannot co_exist at the same time in the same mind. One will dominate and rule the other because they have conflicting interests. With all kinds of battles to be fought and won, it's no wonder that peace is seldom achieved any where. As such, imagine the following conversation between Lucifer and God:

Lucifer: "Give me creative power and authority, God, and I will create things for you to prove how much I love you."

God: "Those are nice thoughts, Lucifer, my brilliant angel, but I know you. I know you better than you think you know yourself. You cannot be trusted with that power and authority. I'll prove it to you! Watch me create planet Earth and everything on it, including people made in my own image. I will give them the ability to pro_create, the closest thing I can give without giving them absolute creative power and ability. Will they be any different than you not having the power and ability to create? I tell you: No! In times to come their pride and self_esteem will likewise cause them to desire the same thing you desire _ to take my place on the throne of the Universe. Little do they realize that without me, life simply cannot exist. They will not be satisfied with me and with pro_creation; they will still desire pure creation that only I possess. In essence, Lucifer, they will be just like you and want me dead so they can have control. You will see all of this come to pass during a period of hundreds and thousands of years. This will be my way of providing evidence that I know what I am talking about. As I have said: 'I tell you now before it happens, so that when it does happen, you will believe.'

"I will give them everything they could possibly want and need, and yet they will not be satisfied. They will blame me for things they assume they do not have. Their desire for things is unlimited, but their real problem is: <u>They don't know me</u>! They want everything I can do for them and everything I can give them, but they do not want me. They really don't want to be my friend; they want me only for selfish reasons. They even claim that they worship me, but in reality they are far from it. Sometimes I get so disgusted. They refuse to listen to me, and then when the going gets rough, they cry on my shoulder and accuse me of not lending a hand. They choose not to listen to me, so I let them go their own way. Sadly, the end result of going their own way is death."

<u>The prophet Amos wrote</u>:

"I hate, I despise your religious feasts. I cannot stand your assemblies. Even though you bring me burnt offerings and grain offerings, I will not accept them. Though you bring choice fellowship offerings, I will have no regard for them. Away with the noise of your songs! I will not listen to the music of your harps. But let justice roll on like a river, righteousness like a never_failing stream!"

Amos 5:21_24.

<u>The prophet Isaiah wrote</u>:

"Justice is driven back, and Righteousness stands at a distance;
Truth has stumbled in the street, Honesty cannot enter."

Isaiah 59:14

Could conditions like those recorded by Amos and Isaiah exist in our world today? Don't they sound terribly harsh especially when considering the quality of current religious gatherings and current religious services that exist locally and via television and the air waves? Immense and beautiful church buildings as well as smaller ones are filled weekly by attending congregations who worship and praise God. The music is fantastic; the décor is astounding; the presentation of the message appealing. How could God not appreciate it? Surely he must be spiritually involved.

But alas! In the last days, the condition of things on planet Earth is not good. The outward appearance detects no flaw, but it's a different story concerning the inside. The inside is where man does his thinking, and it is there that the true intentions of the heart are exposed for God to read. We can fool ourselves, we can fool others, but we can't fool God. He can read our thoughts with precise accuracy and he knows how we would react to future experiences too!

"I tell you before it happens, because their lukewarm Laodicean attitude is pitiful. No one listens! No one hears God's voice! No one opens the door."

(see Rev. 3:20).

Such are the conditions found on planet Earth that exist prior to Christ's return.

Sharing creative powers would mean there would be less and less need for any connection or relationship with the Creator. It is of major importance that the angels needed to see this for themselves and realize that God did the right thing by not giving them any type of creative or pro_creative powers. One only has to look at the human demonstration that God provided as evidence to this fact. It's not a win_win situation. It turns out to be just as God predicted it would be _ a time of straying away from God and a time when the inhabitants of planet Earth would need God only for selfish reasons, where they would try to manipulate and control even the One who initially created all things. Examine the chaos humans have "created" on their own and by themselves!

Itching Ears

"He who has an ear, let him hear what the Spirit says to the churches" of
Ephesus, Smyrna, Pergamon, Thyatira,
Sardis, Philadelphia, and Laodicea.

Revelation 2 – 3.

And the word of the Lord came again to Zechariah:
"This is what the Lord Almighty says:
'Administer true justice; show mercy and compassion to one another.
Do not oppress the widow or the fatherless, the alien or the poor.
In your hearts do not think evil of each other.'
But they refused to pay attention;
stubbornly they turned their backs and stopped up their ears.
They made their hearts as hard as flint and would not listen to the law
or to the words that the Lord Almighty had sent by his Spirit
through the earlier prophets. So the Lord Almighty was very angry.
"When I called, they did not listen; so when they called, I would not listen,"
says the Lord Almighty.

Zechariah 7:8_13

"Preach the word; be prepared in season and out of season;
Correct, rebuke and encourage – with great patience and careful instruction.
For the time will come when men will not put up with sound doctrine.
Instead, to suit their own desires, they will gather around them a great number
of teachers to say what their <u>Itching Ears</u> want to hear.
They will turn their ears away from the truth and turn aside to myths.
But you, keep your head in all situations, endure hardship,
do the work of an evangelist, discharge all the duties of your ministry."

2 Timothy 4:2_5

Can you blame God? I mean, why should he listen to people who call to him when they refuse to listen to him? Like the quote above says: "When I called, they did not listen; so when they called, I would not listen." No one listens; no one pays any attention to what God is trying to communicate to them. Everyone turns a deaf ear. Think about how we are made: human beings have two ears and only one mouth. What does that say? Does it mean we should listen twice as much as expounding our views on someone else? From the standpoint of function, if a perfectly healthy person has all of his senses in tact, it is the ears which are always capable of non_stop performance. By that I mean that the eyes, for instance, can be closed as well as the mouth; the eyes are not always actively engaged in looking at something, nor is the mouth (the vocal chords) continually engaged in dialogue, although there are some, it seems, who try their hardest to prove otherwise!

Listening to God. God wants us to listen to him, but in all actuality, how many people in past history have actually heard God's voice with their own ears? Not very many, I suspect! But God does communicate with everyone who wants to know him, doesn't he? And if he doesn't do it verbally, what procedure is involved? Does he use the Holy Spirit to communicate? Does he use other people in some way?

In the time of Zechariah, the verses quoted above from scripture depict a scene that probably transcends to modern times as well. Hearts hardened as solid as rock (flint) and a refusal to allow their ears to hear any sound by placing their hands over their own ears, limiting any sound waves to enter. It is a scene all too common, especially when considering small children who likewise do not want to hear or listen to their parents. Move your hands and arms, and cover your ears to things you don't want to hear. The ears are so much different than a person's eyes or mouth which can be physically closed purposely when needed, but it can also be stated when dealing with the eyes that the eyes can actually "hear" what is being said, that the eyes can "understand" the expressions being presented. When the volume of sound is hardly perceivable to the ears, the eyes can interpret and relay to the brain what has actually been said. So, then, hearing can also be accomplished through the eyes, so that the deaf can actually "hear" by optical vision. Reading a book is the obvious way for a deaf person to hear someone else. The reverse can also be true, as the blind can actually "see" by sound waves that penetrate the ear drum.

It is a natural phenomenon to close one's eyes to situations one does not wish to acknowledge; to close one's ears to things one does not want to hear; to close one's mind to information one does not want to process. These are choices that we all tend to make while going about our daily lives. Some things we retain due to their importance while other things we discard as irrelevant and not worth the effort and time. And all the while this is going on, God is trying his best to communicate with us. It's not an easy task for God because he gave us the freedom to choose what we believe is important, and if we choose to ignore him, he is left with few alternatives to get our attention.

What does God want from us? What is he after? Has he tried different methods over the centuries and nothing has seemed to work? Why is it that even after the Crucifixion of Jesus there is still the hardened heart of rock that will not listen? It appears the human race has not progressed in a positive manner since day one. Turning the deaf ear is still running rampant today.

When the Apostle Paul wrote those words to Timothy in the first century after Jesus' death it appears that confusion of beliefs existed, and it was Paul's contention that it would not improve in the years to come. Hence, the warning to everyone about unsound doctrine being promoted by men of dubious talent and knowledge, but it is precisely these individuals who want the religious teachers to tell them what they want to hear. And it is easy to understand that these religious teachers, in order to maintain their job and positions, that they would repeat the required and necessary smooth words. The "itching ears" will hear only what is wanted and what is desired to be heard.

Naturally, the tragic part of all of this, according to Paul, is the fact that when this is done, truth becomes lost sight of and in its place man's wisdom appears. This allows room for all kinds of superstitions, for endless man_made rules and regulations, and for make_believe myths that Paul mentions. For the true man of God, it would be no easy task to discern right from wrong as just a little bit of the false mixed with the truth can cause problems of discontent and distrust among the people.

It seems highly improbable for the Apostle Paul to be involved in a matter dealing with the Sanhedrin, the priestly organization, and a man named Stephen. This occurred, of course, before Paul became the Apostle Paul. Previously, he was known as Saul of Tarsus _ a man who relished bringing smoke on the religious community back in the time of the first Century shortly after Jesus' death. During that time period, a man known as Stephen did not have kind words for the ruling religious teachers of the day; in fact, he proceeded to detail their inadequacies by pointing out their involvement in the death of Christ. Rather than admit their guilt, those pious teachers could only express their rage. Stephen met with a thorough dose of jealousy by the priests, due to his wisdom that was led by the Spirit of God.

This episode recorded in Acts 6 & 7 is another example of mature men who would not listen. Even though they were convicted of Stephen's pronouncement upon them, their pride would allow them to go only so far. Stephen was becoming obnoxious and a pain in the side, so they did as all children would do _ they became furious, they gnashed their teeth, and they covered their ears to avoid listening to him any more. The stoning of Stephen by the religious leaders was probably not the first nor the last time something of that nature happened, but it was at this time that the man called Saul of Tarsus consented to Stephen's death. Saul persecuted many individuals in ignorance of God, all because Saul would not listen either. God ultimately had to eliminate Saul's vision in order for Saul to hear and see Jesus. In his blindness, Saul could "see" God as he actually was for the first time, and when his sight was restored three days later, Paul was a different man. His role as persecutor ended; his role as apostle started.

**Claim Jumpers
And
The Rush for Gold**

Claim Jumpers
And
The Rush for Gold

Especially during the mid_19th Century as the progression of people infiltrating and occupying the western landscape of America increased from east to west, many people laid claim to parcels of land acreage, all of which was surveyed, recorded, and filed in appropriate governmental record books. In time, ownership of every square foot of American soil belonged to a private citizen, corporation, investor, or the federal/state government. For some, men would die to own a piece of real estate, no matter what the size, no matter what the cost.

The 1840's and 50's brought with it a stampede of seekers, not only from the eastern portion of the States but from foreign lands as well. Floating on a ship for days on end for the opportunity to search of gold and silver in the mountains of the West was not a concern, and since the railroad was quickly being built to connect the Pacific Ocean with the Atlantic Ocean, there was no lack of movement from East to West.

It took courage to leave all else behind and carry only a pick ax, a shovel, a steel pan, a tin cup, and a few essentials in a sack slung over one's shoulder, but the thought and the chance to "strike it rich" was all that was needed to become part of a vast parade of adventurers. The lure of gold was overwhelming to the point of becoming a major obsession. Never mind the cruel physical labor of a miner, the sweat and the aching back, and never mind the failure of nothing to show for that labor. The prize could be just a few more feet away within some rocky mountainside, and with just one more hearty swing of the pick ax, the vein of gold might be exposed.

First come, first served was the SOP (Standard Operating Procedure) then as it still is in most cases today. There were many incidents, though, where others who arrived later after a claim had been filed on a particular piece of property who became the new property owners. People who fit into that category were often labeled Claim Jumpers. Somehow, it seems, the original owner of the claim disappeared, and after an appropriate period of time the claim was deemed void and declared abandoned. It was then that the record books were altered and new ownership was recorded – all perfectly legal. This was a common event that happened as the United States developed into a civilized nation. At times, it was a battle between individuals as to who owned what, where, and when. And the winner was usually the one with the most wealth and power to accomplish that task. Being in the right place at the right time was helpful.

"The Rush for Gold" in the United States some 150 years ago ended about as abruptly as it had begun. When production of the 'mother lode' ended, the enthusiasm for future mining became history. Very few mines remain viable and productive.

Something similar and yet very different was appearing on the horizon about the same time though. In fact, another "rush for gold" was taking place simultaneously with the one previously mentioned. This particular "rush for gold" was not for the gold found within the mountains of the West, but rather this gold was the gold to be found, of all places, in the Bible. People were searching then as they are searching now for the gold found on the streets of the Holy City, New

Jerusalem, and to possess that gold, many will abandon all they presently have in order to attain ownership of that precious metal. Nothing is of more importance than to be able to walk on those Streets of Gold.

In the realm of religion and Christianity then, there were many who delved into the search for Biblical gold, and the intensity involved doing so was comparable to that of the aforementioned rush for gold in the West. This involvement did not require an actual pick ax, shovel, steel pan, or tin cup, but it did require many thoughtful hours of study and digging in the Scriptures. Being able to find the streets of gold and walk on them was and is the goal for many. There seems to be nothing of more importance to be found.

Today's modern "Claim Jumpers" are not few. There is a broad spectrum of those who claim the gold for themselves and for others too! These persons have staked their claim on something they have done, similar to the original miners who filed a claim at the mining office. The primary claims they make in the realm of religion and Christianity is the fact that they have "been saved," or have been "born again." In all reality, though, it is only just a claim and nothing more, but there seems to be no amount of dialogue that would convince them otherwise. Their claim, they say, has been recorded and filed in the record books of Heaven, and no one, not even God, can eliminate it there. It is permanent!

For those who boldly make these claims of being "born again" or have "been saved," it seems as though they have over_stepped the boundaries of what God is all about. If people can pronounce themselves to have attained this lofty position, what possible and further need is there for God to be involved? Individuals can do it on their own! Is God then required to accept these individuals and allow them access to the streets of gold in Heaven since they have completed the course? Is it a 'done deal' when the process or procedure is completed?

Jesus said in **Mark 11:22** to **"Have faith in God!"** This phrase seems to be important, especially when viewed in the context of claims about oneself. Only God can read the true intent of each heart. How much better would it be to trust him, to believe in him and have faith in him, and to leave that admission of knowledge with him rather than to declare oneself to have that ability?

Lastly, it seems two verses in John's gospel are appropriate to mention at this time. Jesus said it best when he stated the following words:

"If I testify about myself, my testimony is not valid."

John 5:31.

"He who speaks on his own does so to gain honor for himself."

John 7:18.

Heartburn...On the Road to Emmaus

[Luke 24:13_35]

Now that same day, two of them were going to a village called Emmaus, about seven miles from Jerusalem. They were talking with each other about everything that had happened. As they talked and discussed these things with each other, Jesus himself came up and walked along with them; but they were kept from recognizing him.

He asked them, "What are you discussing together as you walk along?"

They stood still, their faces downcast. One of them, named Cleopas, asked him, "Are you only a visitor to Jerusalem and do not know the things that have happened there in these days?"

"What things?" he asked.

"About Jesus of Nazareth," they replied. "He was a prophet, powerful in word and deed before God and all the people. The chief priests and our rulers handed him over to be sentenced to death, and they crucified him; but we had hoped that he was the one who was going to redeem Israel. And what is more, it is the third day since all this took place. In addition, some of our women amazed us. They went to the tomb early this morning but didn't find his body. They came and told us that they had seen a vision of angels, who said he was alive. Then some of our companions went to the tomb and found it just as the women had said, but him they did not see."

He said to them, "How foolish you are, and how slow of heart to believe all that the prophets have spoken! Did not the Christ have to suffer these things and then enter his glory?" And beginning with Moses and all the prophets, he explained to them what was said in all the Scriptures concerning himself.

As they approached the village to which they were going, Jesus acted as if he were going farther. But they urged him strongly, "Stay with us, for it is nearly evening; the day is almost over." So he went in to stay with them.

When he was at the table with them, he took bread, gave thanks, broke it and began to give it to them. Then their eyes were opened and they recognized him, and he disappeared from their sight. They asked each other, "Were not our hearts burning within us while he talked with us on the road and opened the Scriptures to us?"

They got up and returned at once to Jerusalem. There they found the Eleven and those with them, assembled together and saying, "It is true! The Lord has risen and has appeared to Simon." Then the two told what had happened on the way, and how Jesus was recognized by them when he broke the bread.

Generally speaking, when one mentions the physical condition of "heartburn," most times it has a negative connotation attached to it: Someone has over_eaten or overindulged that has caused a burning sensation within the human body, mainly in the area of the heart. And, of course, since the heart is the primary organ of the body, functioning in a proper and stable manner is of vital importance. That's the physical side of what is commonly called "heartburn."

Another side of "heartburn" could be felt in the emotional/spiritual aspect. This is probably what happened to these two disciples, even though the realization of heartburn occurred while they were walking on the road talking with Jesus. This realization became evident as they were breaking bread, but it was the prior conversation while traveling on the road that brought on the "heartburn" condition. What happened to cause this? Did Jesus do it intentionally? What did Jesus do for these two disciples that prompted them to exclaim as they did:

"Were not our hearts burning within us while he talked with us on the road and opened the Scriptures to us?"

Luke 24:32

Somehow it seems appropriate that a discussion concerning "heartburn" would be found in the gospel that was written by a medical doctor. Hence, this episode is part of the gospel according to Luke, the physician. The other three gospels are void of this particular event. Is that significant? Perhaps! But as already mentioned, this case of "heartburn" is not of the physical nature, but nonetheless it is part of Dr. Luke's record of events.

I like the details of stories, such as: the village called Emmaus was about seven miles from Jerusalem. Is this important information? Not really, I suppose, but it does add authenticity to the story. To me, additional description of time and places, etc. makes the event more special as a person can visualize everything more clearly. In this case, since Emmaus is a small obscure little town, knowing it is seven miles from Jerusalem, a reference point can be established. Most everyone has a good idea where Jerusalem is located on the map.

It's the Evidence!

This recorded episode involving Jesus and two disciples is what I would call to be **'a gentle encounter.'** Did Jesus come right out and identify himself to these two men? Did he enter their discussion and then monopolize the conversation? Can't you just picture the three of them on the dirt road to Emmaus, their feet and sandals covered with dust from the road? Are they walking three abreast? Is Jesus in the middle, flanked by the other two? I wonder if they meet others going the opposite direction to Jerusalem. Do they give a hand salute, a wave, or even a nod of acknowledgment? Are the two disciples even aware that they might have met others headed the other way since they can hardly lift their eyes off the ground? I would like to think that surely Jesus would offer a wave or some other kind of greeting to other passersby. Perhaps other people going to Emmaus may have had to go around them because their pace was too slow. I envision them as three men plodding along, totally enveloped in their conversation and oblivious to all else.

How polite can the Creator of the Universe get? He asked them, "What are you discussing together as you walk along?" (vs. 17). If you were the person with all power and all knowledge, is this something you would do? The disciples, though, are full of sadness and are surprised that anyone, including this person who has just joined them on the road, appears to know nothing about recent events that happened in Jerusalem. Jesus replies to their question with another question: "What things?" What of importance is Jesus allowing to happen? Is he trying to discover where the disciples are in their thought system and in their beliefs? Is Jesus giving them the opportunity to convey information? But didn't Jesus know beforehand what they already believed and were discussing? He already knows what's in our minds, doesn't he? Why did he do it this way? Wasn't it for the disciple's benefit that the conversation progressed the way it did?

Did Jesus chide the two men when he said to them in verse 25: "How foolish you are, and how slow of heart to believe all that the prophets have spoken!" Can we find ourselves in the same situations at times that we, too, are "foolish and slow of heart?" Do we also need to be taught by Jesus, and that he begin all over again with Moses and the Prophets? We really aren't any better off than these two, are we? Perhaps in our own lives we have received inaccurate information and need to start over again at square one. This reminds me of the conversation that Jesus had with his own people prior to his death: **It is written in the Prophets, 'They will all be taught by God.' Everyone who listens to the Father and learns from him comes to me." (John 6:45).** That, my friend, is gentle Jesus at work, providing the answer to man's questions. And he does it so perfectly. Meet people where they are; lead them no faster than they can understand! Present the evidence, and allow people to make their own decision whether to accept or reject that information. Fabulous!

I wonder how far Jesus and the other two men walked together. Was it half the distance from Jerusalem to Emmaus (3 ½ miles)? Could it have been perhaps only one mile? Notice how Jesus reacted when they neared the village of the disciples. Did he impose himself on them? Did he ask if they had an extra place to sleep as evening was near at hand? Jesus made no effort to impose himself on them. He does the same with us, doesn't he? We have the choice to extend the invitation to him as well as to others to be our guests. The disciples themselves showed their hospitality by inviting their visitor into their home. Jesus, of course, accepted their request. This important characteristic of Jesus, of God, is worth noting. With unlimited power and unlimited resources at his fingertips, the Creator of the Universe simply waits. How patient and yet how earnest he must be to present evidence about himself, but he knows it is all so futile and in vain unless it is genuinely desired by individuals. It is then that God can present himself in the proper manner, at the appropriate time and the appropriate place. God knows our being, our inner_most thoughts, our likes, our dislikes, and even though we are "foolish and slow of heart to believe," he still stoops to our level and meets us where we are.

Jesus presented evidence through scripture to the disciples while traveling on the road. It would have been so easy for Jesus to initially say to the disciples on the road: "It's me! I'm alive! I've risen from the grave like I said I would!" Instead, Jesus began with Moses and the Prophets. This is amazing but yet so thoughtful that Jesus would start at the beginning with these two disciples and lead them through the Scriptures. How fortunate they were to have God teach them directly, but then that is exactly what God would like to happen with everyone. **"They will all be taught by God." John 6:45.**

As Jesus broke bread with the two disciples, their eyes were suddenly opened, and they recognized him. It seems reasonable to assume that their recognition was based on the visual contact, especially since later on when Jesus made himself known to the larger group of disciples, he displayed his hands and feet for all to see. And like Jesus said to them then, "a ghost does not have flesh and bones as you see I have." (vs. 39). I like to think that when Jesus "took bread, gave thanks, broke it and began to give it to them" (vs. 30), the two disciples recognized him perhaps when he called them by name while distributing the bread. How would a complete stranger know someone else's name unless that stranger was God? This is only speculation on my part, but while traveling on the road, Jesus' voice and mannerisms could have been somewhat more disguised, but when in close quarters around the table, he may have been more normal in conversation and in his tone of voice. Perhaps this aided the disciples in their recognition of Jesus. And it could have been the fact that they finally had made eye contact with their visitor. Perhaps the convincing evidence was when Jesus took the bread, broke it, and then gave some to the pair of men. As noted above, with both hands exposed, the nail scars would have been all too visible.

Anyway, Jesus abruptly disappeared. Why his sudden exit from the scene? Did Jesus complete all that needed to be done at that time? Did he know beforehand that the two men would consider it a must to return to Jerusalem that night and meet with the other disciples? Why wouldn't Jesus want to make the return journey with them since he presented himself to the larger group in Jerusalem as soon as the two disciples arrived?

Heartburn on the road to Emmaus is an interesting episode in the life of Jesus and in the lives of two disciples. It's Jesus at work, meeting people where they are, leading them no faster than they are able to understand, and best of all it is Jesus representing his Father as only he can do.

The Good News.

The Good News is about God, and if we are to take that news to others, it seems as though Jesus' method of calm reasoning from the Scripture that is free of excitement and sensationalism, but at the same time is loaded with evidence quietly presented by the still small voice, that his method will have a lasting, convincing, and meaningful effect.

John 10

The Shepherd and His Flock

This lesson study of John 10 was written by the Author of this book. It is of special interest to him because, as a farmer who has had experience raising and caring for sheep, the Author relates first hand to the characters in this story. Anyone, though, is able to interpret what Jesus is saying about this familiar scene of farm animals and how they are fed and cared for, and how they respond to those who are their guardians. It is this chapter of John that compels the reader to evaluate the relationship between himself and the Shepherd who takes care of him and leads him to 'the green pastures.' In this chapter it also can be seen how this episode reveals information about characters who are not the sheep or the Shepherd, and if the reader of this book will listen carefully as he reads this chapter of John, he will discover what it is that Jesus wants him to learn by telling this story.

This lesson study would be more beneficial if done within a small group where thoughts can be expressed and open discussion can take place.

John 10

The Shepherd and His Flock (1_21).

<u>Verse 1.</u> *"I tell you the truth, the man who does not enter the sheep pen by the gate, but climbs in by some other way, is a thief and a robber."*
1. What does the man (the thief and robber) steal? Who does he steal it from?
2. What is the sheep pen? What kinds of sheep are in the pen?
3. How does the man climb into the sheep pen some other way? Where has the man been and what has he been doing outside the pen?
4. Does the man who is a thief and a robber stay in the sheep pen? What does he do with the items that he has stolen? Does the man ever exit the sheep pen? If so, how?

<u>Verse 2.</u> *"The man who enters by the gate is the shepherd of his sheep."*
1. Jesus states in verse 7 and 9 that he is the gate to the sheep pen. If the shepherd enters the sheep pen by the gate, he must have previously been outside the pen. Where has the shepherd been and what has he been doing outside the pen?

<u>Verse 3.</u> *"The watchman opens the gate for him, and the sheep listen to his voice. He calls his own sheep by name and leads them out."*
1. Who is the watchman that opens the gate? How does he open the gate? Why can't the shepherd open the gate by himself? Does the watchman have any other duties?

<u>Verse 4.</u> *"When he has brought out all his own, he goes on ahead of them, and his sheep follow him because they know his voice."*
1. How do the sheep know the shepherd's voice so well?
2. The shepherd has brought out all of his own. Does that imply other sheep were left behind? Are there other shepherds who enter by the gate and lead their own sheep out?

<u>Verse 5.</u> *"But they will never follow a stranger; in fact, they will run away from him because they do not recognize a stranger's voice."*
1. Who is the stranger? Is he the thief and the robber?
2. Where will the sheep run? Will they run back to the sheep pen?
3. What concerning the stranger's voice don't the sheep recognize? Is it the tone of his voice, the words that he says, the way he says it?

<u>Verse 6.</u> *"Jesus used this figure of speech, but they did not understand what he was telling them."*
1. Why didn't understanding take place?

<u>Verse 7.</u> *"Therefore Jesus said again, 'I tell you the truth, I am the gate for the sheep'."*
1. As with verse 1, why does Jesus say "I tell you the truth?" What does that imply? If someone has been telling "untruths," who would that be?
2. Jesus says he is the gate in verse 7 & 9, and in verse 11 & 14 he says he is the good shepherd. Is this a conflict? Is he both? Explain.

<u>Verse 8.</u> *"All whoever came before me were thieves and robbers, but the sheep did not listen to them."*
1. Who exactly is 'all whoever came before Jesus?' Would it be correct to assume that 'all whoever comes after Jesus' are likewise thieves and robbers?
2. Concerning the thieves and the robbers, why didn't the sheep listen to them?

<u>Verse 9.</u> *"I am the gate; whoever enters through me will be saved. He will come in and go out, and find pasture."*
1. What does 'will be saved' mean? Saved from what?
2. Is 'finding pasture' related to the sheep 'listening to his voice' in verse 3? What constitutes the pasture? Where is it located outside the sheep pen?

<u>Verse 10.</u> *"The thief comes only to steal and kill and destroy; I have come that they may have life, and have it to the full."*
1. What does the thief 'steal, kill, and destroy'? How does he do it?
2. What is the 'life' that the sheep may have? How is it full (unlimited)? Give a full definition of 'life.' Explain how 'receiving life' is related to 'listening.'

<u>Verse 11.</u> *"I am the good shepherd. The good shepherd lays down his life for the sheep."*
1. Does Jesus being the 'good shepherd' imply there are 'bad shepherds'?
2. What does 'laying down his life' do for the sheep? Why does the shepherd lay down his life? What does 'laying down his life' do for sheep that are not of this fold?

<u>Verses 12, 13.</u> *"The hired hand is not the shepherd who owns the sheep. So when he sees the wolf coming, he abandons the sheep and runs away. Then the wolf attacks the flock and scatters it. The man runs away because he is a hired hand and cares nothing for the sheep."*
1. Who is the 'hired hand'? How is he different from the shepherd who owns the sheep? Is he a "bad" shepherd? How does he actually "see" the wolf coming?
2. How does the shepherd 'own the sheep'? Did he buy them or inherit them?
3. Who is the wolf? With what does the wolf attack the flock? What makes the flock scatter? Do the scattered sheep stay together in small groups?
4. Why does the hired hand 'abandon the sheep and run away'? To where does he run? Does he run back to the sheep pen and look for other sheep? Would the hired hand climb into the sheep pen some other way like the thief and the robber?
5. If the hired hand cares nothing for the sheep, why is he involved at all with the sheep? Did someone fail to check his credentials before hiring him?

<u>Verses 14, 15</u>. *"I am the good shepherd; I know my sheep and my sheep know me _ just as the Father knows me and I know the Father _ and I lay down my life for the sheep."*

1. How does Jesus as the good shepherd 'know his sheep,' and how do his sheep 'know him'? This "knowing" is comparable to the Father knowing Jesus, and Jesus knowing the Father. What would be another word or other words for "know?"

2. What is Jesus' life that he lays down? What prompts him to do this? Is it mandatory for him to 'lay it down'? What would happen if he refused?

<u>Verses 16 18</u>. *"I have other sheep that are not of this sheep pen. I must bring them also. They too will listen to my voice, and there will be one flock and one shepherd. The reason my Father loves me is that I lay down my life – only to take it up again. No one takes it from me, but I lay it down of my own accord. I have authority to lay it down and authority to take it up again. This command I received from my Father."*

1. Who are 'the other sheep'? Why are they not part of this sheep pen? Where is Jesus bringing them? When Jesus says 'they too will listen to his voice,' what is Jesus going to tell them? How is Jesus' voice different from the stranger's voice of verse 5?

2. When Jesus lays down his life, does that have anything to do with "I tell you the truth" in verse 1 and 7? Explain.

3. How does Jesus 'take up his life again'? Could Jesus have refused to lay it down in the first place? When Jesus says he 'takes it up again,' does that imply he has done it before? If so, when and where would that have taken place? Explain in depth.

4. When did Jesus receive authority from his Father? What prompted the Father to give him this authority? Could Jesus have abused that authority?

<u>Verses 19 21</u>. *"At these words the Jews were again divided. Many of them said, 'He is demon_possessed and raving mad. Why listen to him? But others said, 'These are not the sayings of a man possessed by a demon. Can a demon open the eyes of the blind'?"*

1. What has Jesus said and done that has made some of the Jews declare him to be demon_possessed and raving mad? Why do other Jews have a contrary opinion? What has caused the division between them? Why is there reference to 'the blind?'

2. Scripture says that "...every city or household divided against itself will not stand." (Matt. 12:25). Is it possible to apply that verse to the people involved here?

The Unbelief of the Jews (22_42).

<u>Verses 22, 23</u>. *"Then came the Feast of Dedication at Jerusalem. It was winter, and Jesus was in the temple area walking in Solomon's Colonnade."*

1. Is it important that the gospel writer John made sure of the location and the time of the year that this exchange took place? Why?

2. King Solomon built the temple at Jerusalem many years previous to this meeting. Does the mention of Solomon have any significance? Why would Jesus use this particular place to dialogue with these people at this time?

<u>Verses 24 30.</u> *"The Jews gathered around him, saying, 'How long will you keep us in suspense? If you are the Christ, tell us plainly.' Jesus answered, 'I did tell you, but you do not believe. The miracles I do in my Father's name speak for me, but you do not believe because you are not my sheep. My sheep listen to my voice; I know them, and they follow me. I give them eternal life, and they shall never perish; no one can snatch them out of my hand. My Father, who has given them to me, is greater than all; no one can snatch them out of my Father's hand. I and the Father are one'."*

1. Why was it so difficult for the Jews to believe that Jesus was the Christ, the Messiah? Jesus said the Jews were 'not his sheep'. Who exactly were his sheep?
2. When and where did Jesus previously tell the Jews that he was the Christ? Did anyone believe then? Besides miracles, what other evidence did Jesus demonstrate?
3. What does it mean 'to believe in Jesus?' What is another word for "believe?"
4. Jesus' sheep 'listen to his voice.' What does Jesus tell them that they need to know? What does Jesus know about them? Why do the sheep follow him?
5. Define the 'eternal life' that Jesus gives. Define 'perish'. Does the phrase 'never perish' imply that those who do not receive 'eternal life' will perish?
6. Why did Jesus emphasize 'listen'? Why is "listening" better than "seeing?" Is Jesus' message more important than miracles, even though it is Jesus who performs the miracles? Why? In your own opinion, what is the greatest miracle that could happen?
7. How is the Father 'greater than all?' What constitutes the 'Father's hand?'
8. Jesus said "I and the Father are one," _ one in what way?

<u>Verses 31 39.</u> *"Again the Jews picked up stones to stone him, but Jesus said to them, 'I have shown you many great miracles from the Father. For which of these do you stone me'? 'We are not stoning you for any of these,' replied the Jews, 'but for blasphemy, because you, a mere man, claim to be God.' Jesus answered them, 'Is it not written in your Law, "I have said you are gods?" If he called them gods, to whom the word of God came – and the scripture cannot be broken _ what about the one whom the Father set apart as his very own and sent into the world? Why then do you accuse me of blasphemy because I said, 'I am God's son'? Do not believe me unless I do what my Father does. But if I do it, even though you do not believe me, believe the miracles that you may know and understand that the Father is in me, and I in the Father.' Again they tried to seize him, but he escaped their grasp."*

1. Why stones? Why didn't Jesus let them stone him then?
2. If the Jews could have been successful in stoning Jesus then, could that death have replaced the Cross? In like manner, what if King Herod's decree to kill all of the infant males two years old and younger had been successful and Jesus' life came to an end at that time. Would his death and spilled blood then have been sufficient? Also, if Jesus had

suffered death due to an accident of some kind, could that death have replaced the Cross? Is the Cross the only adequate method for Jesus to die? Why? Explain.

3. Jesus claimed he was God's Son, the Messiah. Why did the Jews find that so difficult to believe when Old Testament prophecy ('the word of God; the scripture that cannot be broken') pointed directly to Jesus?

4. According to Jewish belief and tradition, blasphemy was deserving of death. Jesus told them not to believe what he says unless he does what his Father does. What specifically is Jesus referring to here about his Father? What does the Father do that Jesus does likewise? Cite reliable evidence that Jesus offers in response to the Jew's accusation. Does the proof that Jesus presents have any effect on their attitude toward him? Why was it so hard for the Jews to believe what Jesus was telling them? Was their decision to reject Jesus due to their state of mind? (see John 9:41; 15:25).

5. Jesus wanted the Jews to 'know and understand that the Father is in him, and that he is in the Father.' When will the fulfillment of that statement be experienced? Does John 14:11, 20 shed any light or have anything to offer in regard to this?

6. Jesus was greatly out_numbered during this entire episode, and again the Jews tried to seize him. How did he escape their grasp? How did he avoid being captured?

<u>Verses 40 42.</u> *"Then Jesus went back across the Jordan to the place where John had been baptizing in the early days. Here he stayed and many people came to him. They said, 'Though John never performed a miraculous sign, all that John said about this man was true.' And in that place many believed in Jesus."*

1. John the gospel writer interjects some information about John the Baptist. Is there a reason for doing so at this particular time? What were the 'true things' that John said about Jesus? Why didn't John the Baptist perform miraculous signs? Was it due to the fact that he knew what he said about Jesus was all that really mattered?

2. What does it mean to 'believe in Jesus?' What did the people who believed in Jesus really believe? What did they accept as truth? Elaborate.

Conclusion:

The example of the shepherd and the sheep should have been readily understood and received by those with whom Jesus dialogued, but such was not the case. Adherence to preconceived thoughts and tradition proved to be a great hindrance to closed_minded people who refused to receive any kind of information contrary to previous teachings. Listening to Jesus reveal information about himself and his Father invoked hatred strong enough to entertain thoughts of death, even to the point of killing the One who claimed to be God's Son. Their hardened and callused minds were not capable of discerning truth, but their minds were capable of eliminating by stoning the person who was turning their belief system upside down, and for people with that kind of mindset, the sooner that Jesus was crucified, the better. Unwilling to listen to Jesus, their minds were filled only with thoughts instilled by Satan, the devil, the father of lies. Jesus' death on the Cross became the result of insane religious people who refused to open their minds to new information that Jesus came to explain and demonstrate.

For us today, how do we "listen" to Jesus? How do we know for sure it is his voice we are following and not that of a 'stranger?' Are we positive that we know who the wolf is? How about the hired hand? Who is the hired hand today; where is he; and what is he doing? Do we believe what Jesus says about the Father is absolutely more important than "modern_day miracles" that are seen in some religious circles today? What unquestionable evidence solidifies our own personal belief in Jesus and his Father?

In the gospel of John, Jesus says "I tell you the truth..." twenty_six times.
Why would Jesus place repeated emphasis on that phrase?

What does it mean to "believe in Jesus?"

CHAPTER 12

A Sword for the Lord...
and for Gideon

A Sword for the Lord...
and for Gideon.

[Judges 7:1_25]

"A Few Good Men"

"Anyone who trembles with fear may turn back and leave Mount Gilead."
So twenty_two thousand men left, while ten thousand remained.
But the Lord said to Gideon, "There are still too many men.
Take them down to the water, and I will sift them for you there.
If I say, 'This one shall go with you,' he shall go;
but if I say, 'This one shall not go with you,' he shall not go."
So Gideon took the men down to the water.
There the Lord told him, "Separate those who lap the water
with their tongues like a dog from those who kneel down to drink."
Three hundred men lapped with their hands to their mouths.
All the rest got down on their knees to drink.
The Lord said to Gideon, "With the three hundred men that lapped
I will save you and give the Midianites into your hands.
Let all the other men go, each to his own place."

Judges 7:3_7

"A Few Good Men."

Most military commanders prepared for battle would always consider an ample number of soldiers is necessary for fighting because, if for no other reason, there are always casualties that decrease the fighting force. The advantage of numbers also has a strategic affect on the opponents who can become very fearful just by observing the overwhelming size of the enemy. Daring men, though, do not consider numbers to be of any advantage; in fact, it can be detrimental in many cases. Such was the case with Gideon who was commissioned by the Lord to drive the Midianites out of the valley near the hill of Moreh.

Three thousand years ago and previous to that, people and nations did not consume each other with the weapons found in the arsenal that most nations possess today. Nuclear bombs, fire power that can be launched from hundreds and even thousands of miles away, rapid_fire explosive devises; these are typical methods of crippling an opponent to the point of extinction, if necessary. Utter annihilation is possible with the use of such weapons. At the time of Gideon, the basic tools for fighting included knives and swords, and this, of course, meant that there was a lot of hand_ to_hand combat taking place. Physical conditioning and training was vital to earning victory over a person's opponent.

This story of Gideon reveals something about God and his method of dealing with the Midianites who were joined by the Amalekites and other eastern people. This group of people had crossed the Jordan River and had camped in the Valley of Jezreel, and it was from this location that Gideon and his army of 32,000 foot soldiers were to evict the intruders. But there was a problem that needed to be corrected: Gideon had too many men! For many individuals involved with fighting that could mean the possibility of death, fear is a factor with which to be reckoned. Emotional control has to be maintained if a soldier is to conquer the enemy, and being afraid has a lot to do with being defeated. Of the original 32,000 men, 22,000 were sent home immediately, leaving 10,000 which is still a sizable number with which to plan and work. But the Lord knows that for all intended purposes a reduction in number will be advantageous. A smaller, efficient army can move about more freely and be less detected than a large contingent. And so, with just 300 men Gideon's army has met the challenge and is ready for battle. Can you picture them there with swords sharpened and ready? Can you picture the scene as Gideon gets them organized and reveals the plan? It must have been a moment of intense excitement.

The Genesis Sword. [Gen. 3:1_24].

The use of swords is mentioned in scripture from Genesis to Revelation. One might truly say that the use of swords was started by the Lord God himself. This occurred, of all places, in the Garden of Eden shortly after "The Fall," the episode where Adam and Eve realized they had been deceived by the serpent. The far_reaching affects of that occurrence introduced the first use of a sword on planet Earth, and at that time Adam and Eve lost something of great importance: access to the Tree of Life. For the pair in the Garden, the fruit from that tree was everything as it provided life in its fullest form: man would live forever! It was the key to perpetual, unending existence! But when the couple listened to the serpent and believed his lies instead of trusting God, there was a change in plans. A flaming sword that was located on the east side of the Garden flashed back and forth and guarded the way to the Tree of Life. Never again would Adam and Eve (or anyone else for that matter) be permitted to dine from the fruits that the tree produced. It was completely off_limits! The obvious question is: Why? The obvious answer is: God was not going to have an immortal sinner on his hands to deal with for all eternity. So what actually happened to the Tree of Life? Could it have been lost in The Flood in the days of Noah? Could it have been preserved in some miraculous way? Is the Tree of Life mentioned again in scripture?

Swords and Words.

Swords and words have similarities: they both can cut. Words spoken in haste and packed with emotion are generally regrettable at a later time. Sometimes, hurting words can cut a person so deep that all the healing in the world cannot mend the situation. Cutting to the bone, words can devastate another person for a lifetime, and repairing that act of violence is a task that is seldom undertaken, and even less seldom accomplished. It's so easy to spit the words out of the mouth, but for the words to return to their origin, it's impossible. In the parable of the Clean and Unclean, Jesus said these words to the crowd: **"Listen and understand. What goes into a** man's mouth does not make him 'unclean,' but what comes out of his mouth, that is what makes him 'unclean'." Matt. 15:10. Normal eating habits include the intake of various foods for the natural maintenance of life which is done effectively by inserting such nourishment into the mouth, chewing, and then swallowing. Digestion will then take place. Doing this procedure is okay and necessary; however, the opposite procedure of expelling words that cause hurt feelings and damage to someone else's well_being can be detrimental, long_lasting, and irreversible. It's possible that such acts are permanently deposited in the memory bank of the receiver.

The Revelation Sword. [Rev. 1:16; 2:12, 16].

The description of someone "like a son of man" found in Revelation 1:12_16 is an awesome picture that portrays this person as having the facial characteristic of "out of his mouth came a sharp double_edged sword." This must be figurative language, of course! The words of Rev. 2:12 concerning the Church in Pergamum coincide with those just mentioned: "These are the words of him who has the sharp, double_edged sword." Can any other conclusion be reached other than swords represent words in these instances?

The Sword of:

Isaiah 49:2 "He made my mouth like a sharpened sword..."

Ezekiel 21:9 "A sword, a sword, sharpened and polished, sharpened for the slaughter, polished to flash like lightning!"

Eph. 6:17 "Take the helmet of salvation and the sword of the Spirit, which is the word of God.

Matt. 10:34 "Do not suppose that I have come to bring peace to the earth. I did not come to bring peace, but a sword."

Matt. 26:52 "Put your sword back in its place," Jesus said to him, "for all who draw the sword will die by the sword."

John 18:11 Jesus commanded Peter, "Put your sword away! Shall I not drink the cup the Father has given me?"

Luke 22:36_38 He said to them, "But now if you have a purse, take it, and also a bag; and if you don't have a sword, sell your cloak and buy one. It is written: 'And he was numbered with the transgressors'; and I tell you that this must be fulfilled in me. Yes, what is written about me is reaching its fulfillment." The disciples said, "See, Lord, here are two swords." "That is enough," he replied.

It seems so contradictory that Jesus, described as the Prince of Peace in Isaiah, makes it known that he "did not come to bring peace, but a sword," a sword that divides everything! Why the apparent discrepancy? Is there confusion on Jesus' part?

Shortly before he was arrested, Jesus instructed Peter to put his sword away because Peter drew his sword and cut off the ear of Malchus, the servant of the high priest. Peter did the wrong thing, but yet Jesus told the disciples to buy a sword even if you have to sell your coat! Are the disciples getting mixed messages from Jesus? What is Jesus after? Are their signals getting crossed? It seems as though no matter what the disciples do it's the wrong thing!

Jesus _ The Word of God.

John 1:1_5. "In the beginning was the Word, and the Word was with God and the Word was God. He was with God in the beginning. Through him all things were made; without him nothing was made that has been made. In him was life, and that life was the light of men. The light shines in the darkness, but the darkness has not understood it."

Heb. 4:12. "For the word of God is living and active. Sharper than any double_edged sword, it penetrates even to dividing soul and spirit, joints and marrow; it judges the thoughts and attitudes of the heart."

Both the sword and the word do their intended purpose, and the result is clearly seen. There's no escape from the word of God as it cuts through all the red tape and the illusions of the mind; it gets to the bottom of things quickly! All of the masks that are worn from time to time are stripped of their cover_up appearance when the sword and the word are combined. What is visualized then is the stark reality of everyone's personal character, fully exposed for all to see. There are no hiding places where traits can be buried and forgotten.

Returning to Gideon's battle with the Midianites, three hundred men of God's choosing routed an immense number of opponents. At night carrying jars, with torches in their left hands and with trumpets in their right hands, and with a shout, **"A sword for the Lord and for Gideon,"** an over_whelming number of enemies died by the sword _ their own sword! Like the scripture says, "All who draw the sword will die by the sword." It would have been better if the episode with Gideon had ended in a respectable way, but such was not the case. Idol worship of gold figurines followed in the aftermath of a victorious battle won by just three hundred men.

Although the Tree of Life, whose fruit made it possible for life as we know it to never end, was placed out_of_bounds to our first parents in the Garden of Eden, the same Tree of Life appears again in the book of Revelation. Three times it is mentioned in Genesis; three times in Revelation. It is with joy and great anticipation that once again the Tree of Life will provide the nourishment to sustain life for all eternity.

Sword and Words.

Notice the spelling of both words.
Take the "s" from sword and move it to the other side of "d" and it spells words.
The reverse is likewise true:
Take the "s" from words and move it to the other side of "w" and it spells sword!

Guarding the Yeast

<u>Matthew 16:1 12.</u>

The Pharisees and Sadducees came to Jesus and tested him by asking him to show them a sign from heaven. He replied, "When evening comes, you say, 'It will be fair weather, for the sky is red,' and in the morning, 'Today it will be stormy, for the shy is red and overcast.' You know how to interpret the appearance of the sky, but you cannot interpret the signs of the times. A wicked and adulterous generation looks for a sign, but none will give it except the sign of Jonah." Jesus then left them and went away.

When they went across the lake, the disciples forgot to take bread. "Be careful," Jesus said to them. "Be on your guard against the yeast of the Pharisees and Sadducees." They discussed this among themselves and said, "It is because we didn't bring any bread."

Aware of their discussion, Jesus asked, "You of little faith, why are you talking among yourselves about having no bread? Do you still not understand? Don't you remember the five loaves for the five thousand, and how many basketsful you gathered? How is it you don't understand that I was not talking to you about bread? But be on your guard against the yeast of the Pharisees and Sadducees."

Then they understood that he was not telling them to guard against the yeast used in bread, but against the teaching of the Pharisees and Sadducees.

Four thousand people, not including women and children, were fed with seven loaves of bread and a few small fish. Jesus had somehow been able to curb the gnawing appetite of this group of people with an initial small portion of available food. For the people and the disciples, no doubt it was a miracle of some sort, but even more improbable was the amount of leftovers _ seven full baskets. Think of the number of people Jesus could have blessed with a full stomach distributing the food from seven baskets at a later time! The tally could have been immense. It's not detailed in the scriptures, but I often wonder what happened to the leftovers the next day and who took charge of the residue of food. This episode immediately precedes the Biblical verses written above.

Leave it up to the religious community of the day to test Jesus: they want a miraculous sign from heaven to prove he was the person he claimed to be. Evidently, the bread and fish demonstration did nothing for them, even though the quantity of food was multiplied many times over. Jesus showed them their true position by revealing how they were able to discern the clouds in the sky, but were unable to discern the presence of God in their midst. Jesus gave them a clue by referring to Jonah, the prophet. Jonah spent three days inside the fish; Jesus, three days in the tomb. The group of Pharisees and Sadducees seen here was similar to the people of Nineveh to which Jonah was instructed to witness. It's hard to believe that 120,000 people there could not tell their right hand from their left.

Religious instructions were mandated from one generation of Pharisees and Sadducees to the next. It seemed as though the attitude of: "It was good enough for Grandpa; it's good enough for me!" prevailed. The teachings, the doctrines that they had applied equally as well to following generations, so why even think about something else? Just continue to use the same yeast in the bread as always. It was good for them; it will be good for us too! Such was the mindset for the religious community, and faithfully guarding that yeast was committed to their belief system. It was a closed_minded attitude!

Jesus, on the other hand, had something to say about the yeast (the leaven) of the Pharisees and Sadducees: "Avoid it like the plague!" Jesus' mission with the disciples for three years included the warning to beware of the teachings and doctrines that enshrouded the religious community in a cloud of false information. While teaching those who were willing to listen, Jesus offered little acknowledgement of anything positive or true concerning the beliefs of the religious community, and for all practical purposes it was useless to try to communicate and reason with them because Jesus knew their true intent was to eliminate him. Twice, in verses 6 and 11, Jesus warned the disciples to be on their guard against the yeast used by the Pharisees and Sadducees in this verbal exchange. Perhaps today's followers of Christ should likewise heed the same warning concerning present_day yeast. **"Be on your guard!"**

The gospel of Luke contains further warning about the yeast of the Pharisees as the following words of Jesus demonstrate:

"Be on your guard against the yeast of the Pharisees, which is hypocrisy. There is nothing concealed that will not be disclosed, or hidden that will not be made known. What you have said in the dark will be heard in the daylight, and what you have whispered in the ear in the inner rooms will be proclaimed from the roofs."

Luke 12:1_3

Yeast, according to Jesus in this passage, is hypocrisy. The teachings and the doctrines promoted by that religious group have some serious flaws, and Jesus wants that information to be made known to everyone. As yeast, the incorrect information has permeated the entire realm of thought concerning God and what God is all about. It is Jesus' contention that there is great need to **"be on your guard against the yeast"** that has led many astray with misconceptions. We all would do well to heed Jesus' advice and be sure that we do not partake of that yeast. The ending to this passage in Luke evidently concerns those persons who have not allowed the yeast to saturate their minds:

"When you are brought before synagogues, rulers and authorities, do not worry about how you will defend yourselves or what you will say, for the Holy Spirit will teach you at the time what you should say."

Luke 12:11, 12

Words of confidence like those above will sustain those who refuse to partake in the yeast offered by the religious community of the day.

Giving the Gift

[Two Demonstrations]
(followed by reading 5 verses from John's gospel).

Demonstration #1.

Object involved: A gift.
Characters involved: One Giver; One Receiver.
    The Giver: Any person with a gift.
    The Receiver: Any person wanting the gift.
Place of Demonstration: The Receiver's home.
Time of Demonstration: Important Event, i.e. Christmas, Birthday, Graduation.

The Conversation:
Giver to Receiver: "I've come to your home today to give you this gift. I understand that you have wanted this particular gift for quite some time. It gives me a great deal of pleasure and it makes me happy that I am able to present this gift to you.
Giver places "the gift" in Receiver's hands.

Conversation continues:
Giver to Receiver: "Now that I've given you this gift, I've finished what I came to do, so I'm going to return to my home. You may open this gift after I leave to go straight home."
Giver leaves. Receiver opens gift. It is exactly what the Receiver wanted. Nothing the Giver could have given him would have made the Receiver happier. This is the ultimate gift that the Receiver desired.

Demonstration #2.

Object involved: A Gift.
Characters involved: One Giver; One Receiver.
    The Giver: God, with a Gift.
    The Receiver: Any person wanting the Gift.
Place of Demonstration: The Receiver's home.
Time of Demonstration: Any time the Receiver is willing to accept the Gift.

<u>The Conversation:</u>

God to any person wanting the Gift: "I've come to your home today to give you this Gift. I understand that you have wanted this particular Gift for quite some time. It gives me a great deal of pleasure and I am most happy that I am able to present this Gift to you. I want you to know that I don't expect anything in return, because I am perfectly willing to give you this Gift with no strings attached. I give it to you because I know that you want it. If you didn't want it, I wouldn't be giving it to you."

God gives Gift to the Receiver.

<u>Conversation continues:</u>

God, the Giver to the Receiver: "Now that you have received this Gift, I have finished what I came to do, so I'm going to return home, knowing that you are happy with my Gift to you. I'm positive this is the ultimate Gift you have always wanted. You may open your Gift now, and as you do, I'll be on my way. I want you to know that I am going to Calvary first, and then I'll go straight home."

Receiver opens the Gift... of Eternal Life!

<u>John 17:1 5</u>. Jesus' Prayer to His Father.

After Jesus said this, he looked toward heaven and prayed:

Father, the time has come. Glorify your Son, that your Son may glorify you. For you granted him authority over all people that he might give eternal life to all those you have given him. <u>Now this is eternal life: that they may know you, the only true God, and Jesus Christ, whom you have sent</u>. I have brought you glory on earth by completing the work you gave me to do. And now, Father, glorify me in your presence with the glory I had with you before the world began.

<u>Jesus' Work</u>: Giving the Gift of Eternal Life.

Jesus' death on the Cross was not the Work he came to do, but was the result of the impact he had on people's lives. Jesus' Work was to reveal his Father, to give information about him to those willing to receive it. The giving of this gift was completed before Jesus died on the Cross. (John 17:4). The rejection of that information by those not willing to receive it is what caused Jesus' death. They could only shout. "He is demon_possessed and raving mad! Crucify him! Crucify him!"

For those who desire to receive the information about God from Jesus, it becomes "living water" from a spring that wells up to eternal life. (John 4:14). It is Eternal Life!

Eternal Life is knowledge (correct knowledge) about God. (John 17:3). Jesus is the only One who has the authority to give this gift.

Eternal Life is received when individuals believe the information that Jesus reveals about his Father. (John 6:63).

Whoever believes in the Son has eternal life. (John 3:36).

For God so loved the world that he <u>gave</u> his one and only Son... *(What did the Father give his Son? He gave him authority to represent him!),* **that whoever believes in him shall not perish but have eternal life (the correct knowledge about God). (John 3:16).** *Believe what Jesus says about his Father equals Eternal Life!*

For God did not send his Son into the world to condemn the world, but to save the world through him. (John 3:17). *Salvation (Eternal Life) is based upon what Jesus has made known about his Father, what he has demonstrated for all to see. It is not dependant upon what happens at Calvary.*

Calvary demonstrates the insanity of sin, that sin's goal is to kill the One who is willing to give life to everyone. The work that Jesus came to do was not to die on the Cross. His death was the result of the impact that the information he made known about his Father had on those who refused to accept what he revealed and demonstrated. Jesus' work was completed when he offered the gift of eternal life and it was accepted by those willing to receive it. How totally happy Jesus must have been when he exclaimed to his disciples: "You believe at last!" (John 16:31). What did the disciples finally believe? They believed the evidence concerning God that Jesus presented to them. When that happened, Jesus was willing to travel to Calvary, knowing that he had fulfilled his mission. When Jesus spoke the words: "It is finished," the unmistakable characteristics of Satan, the father of lies and a murderer from the beginning, were fully exposed. Who, besides Satan the devil, would seek to kill the One who gives life? The answer: only insane religious people who have the wrong picture of God!

**Jesus demonstrated the truth about God, his heavenly Father,
with unquestionable evidence.**

**Jesus demonstrated the truth about Satan, the adversary,
by revealing his true nature and character as one whose ultimate goal
was to kill the Life_Giver, God.**

The Damascus Road

[Acts 9:1_19]

Meanwhile, Saul was still breathing out murderous threats against the Lord's disciples. He went to the high priest and asked him for letters to the synagogues in Damascus, so that if he found any there who belonged to the Way, whether men or women, he might take them as prisoners to Jerusalem. As he neared Damascus on his journey, suddenly a light from heaven flashed around him. He fell to the ground and heard a voice say to him, "Saul, Saul, why do you persecute me?"

"Who are you, Lord?" Saul asked.

"I am Jesus, whom you are persecuting," he replied. "Now get up and go into the city, and you will be told what you must do."

The men traveling with Saul stood there speechless; they heard the sound but did not see anyone. Saul got up from the ground, but when he opened his eyes he could see nothing. So they led him by the hand into Damascus. For three days he was blind, and did not eat or drink anything.

In Damascus there was a disciple named Ananias. The Lord called to him in a vision, "Ananias!"

"Yes, Lord," he answered.

The Lord told him. "Go to the house of Judas on Straight Street and ask for a man from Tarsus named Saul, for he is praying. In a vision he has seen a man named Ananias come and place his hands on him to restore his sight."

"Lord," Ananias answered, "I have heard many reports about this man and all the harm he has done to your saints in Jerusalem. And he has come here with authority from the chief priests to arrest all who call on your name."

But the Lord said to Ananias, "Go! This man is my chosen instrument to carry my name before the Gentiles and their kings and before the people of Israel. I will show him how much he must suffer for my name."

Then Ananias went to the house and entered it. Placing his hands on Saul, he said, "Brother Saul, the Lord – Jesus, who appeared to you on the road as you were coming here – has sent me so that you may see again and be filled with the Holy Spirit." Immediately, something like scales fell from Saul's eyes, and he could see again. He got up and was baptized, and after taking some food, he regained his strength.

One can only imagine the magnitude of the meeting on the road to Damascus that day, and for Saul of Tarsus, this had to be an eye_opening experience once the veil of blindness was lifted from his eyes. Was there no other way that he could have received the "light of truth" from a God that he methodically and mistakenly persecuted? Had his incorrect beforehand vision so permeated his entire being, his mind, and his actions that there was no alternative left for God to use? Why three days of blindness? Wouldn't just one or two have been sufficient? Why would the God of Heaven choose a man of Saul's reputation to be an instrument that would later proclaim the Lord's name? Lastly, how could God watch with intensity and yet not interfere with the stoning death of Stephen, and then shortly thereafter recruit Saul of Tarsus who gave his personal approval of Stephen's death? What does that say about God? Can a God like that be trusted?

I admire the man Saul of Tarsus, even before he became Paul the Apostle. Here was a man of confidence, of one who believed that what he was doing was the right thing. He was bold; he was energetic; he was feared. He possessed the ability to persevere in all situations, even when things weren't going his way. He would not take no for an answer, but would relentlessly press on until the job was completed. But Saul had a major flaw: he was in complete opposition to God.

When I read about the man Ananias and the vision that was given to him, how many of us today would be willing to obey the Lord and confront someone similar to Saul's reputation? Would we try to find some excuse? Would we totally resist? It appears from the record that there was apprehension on the part of Ananias, and rightly so! It would seem logical and reasonable to question everything about the vision that was presented to him, but when the Lord says "Go," the man of God resists no longer. Ananias travels to Straight Street in Jerusalem and finds the man named Saul of Tarsus. Having never met Saul previously, it seems highly improbable that when Ananias first greeted him that he would call him Brother Saul. Even so, Saul immediately received his sight and became filled with the Holy Spirit. What does this say about God? Does God intend for everyone to learn an important lesson from this? What are we to 'take home and study' from this episode? Only God can accurately read the heart and the intentions of the heart and mind, but couldn't he have found a more worthy candidate than a rebel like Saul? One can only surmise from this brief encounter that God knows what he is doing.

Can we know from God's view point how the character of Saul was the one most needed at that time to represent the Creator of the Universe? Why was Saul the chosen instrument when there were an ample number of learned scholars available to represent God? Why not select someone who, at least, was thought to be on God's side? Perhaps that was a problem then. Perhaps many appeared to be on God's side, but only a few had the right view of God. The conversion of Saul to Paul is so dramatic that even Jesus' disciples stood in awe at the power of God. Who can argue with evidence like this? One can only be amazed how God can so quickly and thoroughly influence and change a person's attitude and mind. What happened to Saul on the Damascus Road provides evidence in the manner that God can and will work with individuals. It can also be seen with Ananias that God knows and will use those who trust him to participate in events that bring glory to God.

Please Pass the Mustard, John!

Strange as it may seem, the Parable of the Mustard Seed is omitted in John's gospel. In fact, John's gospel contains hardly any parables compared to that of Matthew, Mark and Luke. Nonetheless, this article is entitled the way it is. For purposes later to be exposed, the <u>Must</u> in the <u>Must</u>ard is the main topic of discussion contained within. The parable as found in Matthew is copied below:

<u>The Parable of the Mustard Seed.</u>

He (Jesus) told them another parable: "The kingdom of heaven is like a mustard seed, which a man took and planted in his field. Though it is the smallest of all your seeds, yet when it grows, it is the largest of garden plants and becomes a tree, so that the birds of the air come and perch in its branches.

Matt. 13:31, 32

Plant a very small seed, in fact, the smallest of all seeds, and expect humongous results: a plant of large stature that is capable of being the resting place for birds. It seems as though a true farmer, and a gardener as well, would include planting at least one mustard seed in his field/garden each year, not only for birds to take a rest from flight, but more importantly to remind the farmer/gardener that the kingdom of heaven is compared to this tiny seed. It may start out small, but the end result is fantastic! That tiny seed becomes a tree! Would it be okay to say that planting a <u>must</u>ard seed is a <u>must</u>?

John's <u>Mustard</u> Seed

From what I have searched and read from John's version of the gospel, the <u>Must</u> is more important than the Mustard! With that in mind, the journey through this book of the Bible begins in chapter three with the clandestine meeting of Jesus and Nicodemus and will end with verse twenty two in the last chapter of John.

When someone is told that he/she <u>must</u> do something, does that mean it is an order? Also, could <u>must</u> possibly mean that it is a plea? And lastly, could <u>must</u> be an imperative, similar to an order? Could any of these definitions of <u>must</u> have anything to do with the kingdom of Heaven, as stated in the mustard parable?

<u>Chapter 3.</u>

**Jesus answered, "I tell you the truth, no one can enter the kingdom
of God unless he is born of water and the Spirit.
Flesh gives birth to flesh, but the Spirit gives birth to spirit.
You should not be surprised at my saying,
'You <u>must</u> be born again'."**

John 3:5_7

It appears from this sentence that as Jesus spoke to Nicodemus, it is imperative, for him at least, to be born again, especially in light of previous verse three where Jesus first tells Nicodemus another "truth."

**Jesus declared, "I tell you the truth, no one can see the kingdom of God
unless he is born again."**

John 3:3

Jesus seems to emphasize to Nicodemus two main items: "I tell you the truth," and the need to be "born again." And unless Nicodemus understands this, he cannot "see" the kingdom of God. This "seeing," as I visualize it, does not involve actual sight, but rather the ability to understand, to "see" what someone else is talking about. Hence, Nicodemus <u>must</u> understand what Jesus is telling him in these verses, and yet more importantly, he <u>must</u> understand what Jesus is about to tell him as another "truth" in verses following.

Previous verses three and seven concluded that Nicodemus <u>must</u> be born again, especially if he wants to "see" the kingdom of God. Nicodemus does not understand what Jesus is talking about, so he asks the innocent question: "How can this be?" (v.9). Jesus then tells him the answer to his question in the next five verses, and then further explains to the night_time visitor exactly what "earthly things" and "heavenly things" are all about.

"You are Israel's teacher/' said Jesus, "and you do not understand these things?
I tell you the truth, we speak of what we know, and we testily to what we have seen,
but still you people do not accept our testimony.
I have spoken to you of earthly things and you do not believe;
how then will you believe if I speak of heavenly things? No one has gone into heaven
except the one who came from heaven – the Son of Man.
Just as Moses lifted up the snake in the desert, so the Son of Man <u>must</u> be lifted up,
that everyone who believes in him may have eternal life.

John 3:10_15

"Just as Moses lifted up the snake in the desert, so the Son of Man <u>must</u> be lifted up, that everyone who believes in him may have eternal life." Why did Jesus revert back to that particular time and place in history to describe to Nicodemus about snakes? What do snakes have to do with the Son of Man being 'lifted up' and having eternal life? What is the connection, and what should Nicodemus learn from this? The story of Moses and the snake in the desert is found in Numbers 21.

The Bronze Snake.

They traveled from Mount Hor along the route to the Red Sea,
to go around Edom. But the people grew impatient on the way;
they spoke against God and against Moses, and said:
"Why have you brought us up out of Egypt to die in the desert?
There is no bread! There is no water! And we detest this miserable food!"

Then the Lord sent venomous snakes among them; they bit the people
and many Israelites died. The people came to Moses and said,
"We sinned when we spoke against the Lord and against you.
Pray that the Lord will take the snakes away from us."
So Moses prayed for the people.

The Lord said to Moses, "Make a snake and put it up on a pole;
anyone who is bitten can look at it and live."
So Moses made a bronze snake and put it up on a pole.
Then when anyone was bitten by a snake and looked at the bronze snake,
he lived.

Numbers 21:4_9

From the time of Moses, it is much later in history that the Son of Man is actually "lifted up" from the Earth, signifying, of course, the Cross and the Crucifixion. Most of the people under Moses' leadership were grumblers _ no bread; no water; and they detested the manna from heaven.

In short, they were not happy campers while in the wilderness. With an attitude like that, the Lord decided to "send in the snakes!" It was then that Moses made the bronze snake on the pole for all to see.

What a strange parody! Venomous snake bite required that the person bitten by a snake needed to look to another snake on a pole in order to live. What was biting and killing people was actually the same thing that saved them if they took their eyes off the ground with the snakes, and looked to the pole with a bronze snake on it! This seems so absurd! What's the point? Could it be with Nicodemus that eyes <u>must</u> be shifted away from things that were 'killing them' (such as wrong information about God), and be lifted upward to who it is that gives them life and saves them from dying?

It appears from the scripture record that Nicodemus did not have his act together as he thought he did! Even though he was a learned religious scholar, according to Jesus he knew very little about "earthly things," so that left little doubt that he knew anything about "heavenly things." He needed instruction immediately, and Jesus was willing to work with him and explain what was necessary for him (as well as for us) to know. Jesus began his discussion with Nicodemus by making his opening statement about God, which is none other than John 3:16 _ probably the most well_known verse of the Bible.

The gospel of John records two other references to Jesus being "lifted up."

> **They did not understand what he was telling them about his Father.**
> **So Jesus said, "When you have lifted up the Son of Man,**
> **then you will know that I am the one I claim to be**
> **and that I do nothing on my own but speak just what the Father has taught me."**
> **John 8:27, 28**

> **"Now is the time for judgment on this world;**
> **now the prince of this world will be driven out.**
> **But I, when I am lifted up from the earth, will draw all men to myself."**
> **John 12:31, 32**

Nicodemus did not understand what Jesus was talking about in chapter three: "<u>You are Israel's teacher</u>," said Jesus, "<u>and do not understand these things</u>?" John 3:10.

Neither did **the Jews** understand what Jesus was talking about in chapter eight: "<u>They did not understand that he (Jesus) was telling them about his Father.</u>" John 8:27.

The Greeks, the Pharisees, and the Jewish crowd did not understand in chapter twelve that it was judgment time _ a time to decide, to make the judgment, whether to accept Jesus or reject him, because Jesus, 'the light,' would be with them but for 'a little while longer.' (v.35). "<u>But because of the Pharisees they would not confess their faith for fear they would be put out of the synagogue; for they loved praise from men more than praise from God.</u>" John 12:42, 43.

Chapter Four.

**"Sir," the woman said, "I can see that you are a prophet.
Our fathers worshiped on this mountain, but you Jews claim
that the place where we <u>must</u> worship is in Jerusalem."**

John 4:20

The woman at the well is certainly an honest person as this noon_time encounter with Jesus depicts. Although her reputation is questionable, Jesus does not consider that nor her nationality to be a barrier for discussion with her. It is interesting that she says the bold statement she does about the place where Jews <u>must</u> worship (in Jerusalem), especially since she, a Samaritan woman, is not even supposed to talk with Jews, and she knows quite well that Samaritans should avoid interaction with Jews. Why <u>must</u> Jews worship in Jerusalem? Is it due to the importance of Solomon's Temple, at least what's left of it?

In the verses immediately following John 4:20, Jesus comments to the Samaritan woman about where Jews <u>must</u> worship. What's important, Jesus says, is not *where* a person worships, but *how* a person worships.

**Yet a time is coming and has now come when the true worshipers
will worship the Father in spirit and truth, for they are the kind worshipers
the Father seeks. God is spirit, and his worshipers <u>must</u> worship him
in spirit and in truth.**

John 4:24

True worshipers <u>must</u> worship God in spirit and in truth; location of worship is not the issue. In essence, Jesus told the woman that the Samaritans were wrong in their belief that they needed to worship God on that particular mountain, and identically, the Jews were wrong in their belief that they needed to worship in Jerusalem. Both groups had the wrong picture of worship.

Could it be that what Jesus is referring to is that maintaining a certain attitude determines if a person is worshiping God in an acceptable manner, and it is not a person's performance that has meaning to worship? Are true worship and prayer tied together? Do obedience and/or the willingness to listen fit into any of this?

Chapter Six.

**Then they asked him, "What <u>must</u> we do to do the works God requires?"
Jesus answered. "The work of God is this:
to believe in the one he has sent"**

John 6:28

Previous to this question, the people who asked Jesus this question were part of the large group of 5,000 whom Jesus had fed with five loaves of bread and a couple of fish. The next day, on the other side of the Sea of Galilee, the same people were again searching for Jesus, but what they wanted from him was, again, food. Jesus knew this so he said to them: "Do not work for food that spoils, but for food that endures to eternal life, which the Son of Man will give you. On him God the Father has placed his seal of approval." John 6:27. This statement by Jesus was followed by their <u>must</u> question quoted above.

What <u>must</u> they do to do the works God requires? In verse 27 Jesus told them to "work for food that endures to eternal life." This food is none other than information about God that Jesus is willing to freely give them. They only have to be willing to listen to Jesus tell them, and believe what he is telling them is the truth!

Chapter Nine.

**As he went along, he (Jesus) saw a man blind from birth. His disciples
asked him, "Rabbi, who sinned, this man or his parents, that he was born blind?"
"Neither this man nor his parents sinned," said Jesus, "but this happened
so that the work of God might be displayed in his life.
As long as it is day, we <u>must</u> do the work of him who sent me.
Night is coming, when no one can work."**

John 9:3, 4

Jesus encounters a man who was born blind. Although the perceived attitude by other people about someone in that condition meant 'someone must be guilty of sin,' Jesus would have nothing to do with that mindset. Instead, Jesus verbalizes what <u>must</u> be done: restore sight to the blind, because this was the work that the Father sent Jesus to do. The blind man receiving his sight is very similar to Nicodemus "seeing" the kingdom of God. And the act of Nicodemus being "born again" is very similar to the blind man being able to "see" for the first time. This story of the blind man illustrates in the end who the "blind" people really are, and in comparison to the Nicodemus story, the nighttime visit with Jesus illustrates who the people are that need to be "born again." Jesus gives "sight" to Nicodemus by revealing truth about God, and to the man born blind Jesus gives new life and information about God, like being "born again."

Chapter Ten.

**I am the good shepherd; I know my sheep and my sheep know me – just as
the Father knows me and I know my Father – and I lay down my life for the sheep.
I have other sheep that are not of this sheep pen. I <u>must</u> bring them also.
They too will listen to my voice, and there shall be one flock and one shepherd.**

John 10:14_16

Sheep; The Sheep Pen; The Shepherd; The Gate; Thieves and Robbers; The Hired Hand; A Wolf. All of these characters constitute the cast for Jesus' story about "listening." All of Jesus' sheep, whether from this particular sheep pen or not, have one common thread, and that would be listening to Jesus' voice and knowing that it is he who is speaking. They follow him because they know his voice, and they will never follow a stranger because they do not recognize a stranger's voice. Fact is, Jesus' sheep will run the other way! And the hired hand is just that _ a hired hand who has no personal interest in any of the sheep. When left with a hired hand, the sheep are easily attacked by the wolf, and the sheep become scattered.

For Jesus and his sheep, they know each other because they have spent time together. Besides providing pasture and a cool stream of water, Jesus will do just about anything for them because they are his sheep and he is their shepherd. Jesus said: "I have other sheep that are not of this sheep pen. I <u>must</u> bring them also." Who are these sheep of another sheep pen, and where is he going to bring them? Will he bring them to the same pasture to graze and eat, and to drink from the same stream of refreshing water? Relating this to human beings, does this eating and drinking represent the daily task of receiving nourishment to survive? And in the spiritual realm, is this the consumption of information and knowledge about God? All of the sheep listen to his voice, and they will be one flock guided and fed by only one shepherd. Jesus <u>must</u> bring them to unity.

<u>Chapter Twelve.</u>

> **Whoever serves me <u>must</u> follow me; and where I am, my servant also will be.**
> **My Father will honor the one who serves me.**
>
> **John 12:26**

Like the sheep of chapter ten who follow the shepherd because they know his voice, those who serve Jesus do the same. Enthusiasm is a wonderful trait if it is kept in perspective and maintained in an orderly manner. To be of service to someone else means that person understands what the other person verbalizes and demonstrates. In the case of serving Jesus, it is, as Jesus states, a priority to allow Jesus to instruct in such a manner that understanding takes place.

> **The crowd spoke up, "We have heard from the Law that the Christ**
> **will remain forever, so how can you say, 'The Son of Man <u>must</u> be lifted up?'**
> **Who is this Son of Man?"**
>
> **John 12:34**

Jesus told the crowd around him this verse shortly after explaining why they <u>must</u> follow him. Why is it imperative that the Son of Man be "lifted up?" As verses 30_32 explain, when that happens Jesus will draw all men (including angels as well as men) to himself And as this happens, it will be a time for judgment, a time for making a decision whether to accept Jesus or reject him. This question of "how can you say, 'The Son of Man <u>must</u> be lifted up?' reverts back to the passage with Nicodemus when Jesus himself said "the Son of Man <u>must</u> be lifted up, that everyone who believes in him may have eternal life." Nicodemus of chapter three would have had to have passed on those words to others in order for them to say to Jesus what he said previously to Nicodemus.

Chapter Fourteen.

> "You have heard me say, 'I am going away and I am coming back to you.'
> If you loved me, you would be glad that I am going to the Father,
> for the Father is greater than I.
> I have told you now before it happens, so that when it does happen,
> you will believe.
> I will not speak with you much longer, for the prince of this world is coming.
> He has no hold on me, but the world <u>must</u> learn that I love the Father
> and that I do exactly what my Father has commanded me."
>
> John 14:28, 29

The Perfect Relationship

> The Father loves the Son and has placed everything in his hands.
>
> John 3:35

and

> The Son loves the Father and does whatever the Father tells him to do.
>
> John 14:31

The world <u>must</u> learn that the Son is not here on planet Earth to do whatever he wants to do. Jesus never acts alone, and neither would he say anything unless he and the Father were in total agreement. The world <u>must</u> learn the importance of the unity that exists between the Father and the Son.

Chapter Fifteen.

> Remain in me, and I will remain in you.
> No branch can bear fruit by itself; it <u>must</u> remain in the vine.
> Neither can you bear fruit unless you remain in me.
>
> John 15:4

The connection of branches and vines is needed if any fruit is to appear. Not only is this required in the plant world, it also is true in the realm of human beings and their connection to their Creator. Human survival and the need for a relationship with the Divine demands that the branches remain attached to the vine all of the time. There would be no fruit unless there was the existence of mutual dependency. Such is the case with our Creator and with us, his creatures. If we, being the branches, have no connection with God who is the vine, there is no way the branch can produce fruit. This is emphasized in verse five as Jesus says: "apart from me you can do nothing." Nothing will be the outcome when there is no connection between branch and vine. Bearing fruit means being willing to extend the correct picture of God to others, just as Jesus did.

> **When the Counselor comes, whom I will send to you from the Father,**
> **the Spirit of truth who goes out from the Father,**
> **he will testify about me.**
> **And you also <u>must</u> testify, for you have been with me from the beginning.**
> **John 15:26, 27**

This verse is very compelling, especially since it seems quite personal, and perhaps since it is that way, it is daunting and challenging, with a little apprehension thrown into the mix. The thought of testifying about God can be emotional mentally, physically and spiritually. Why is it necessary that the disciples (I assume that means us as well) testify? The previous verse has already stated that the Counselor, the Holy Spirit, will testify about Jesus. Isn't that enough? Surely he can do a much better and a more thorough job than any of us could imagine. Why us? We would surely make a mess of things, wouldn't we? Why does God need our testimony?

Personal testimony could probably happen in a number of ways, but it seems that certain criteria would have to be met by all methods. Could that be the same criteria that John quoted Jesus saying 26 times in this gospel: "I tell you the truth...?" And since Jesus' mission was to 'make his Father known,' it's possible that every time Jesus started dialogue with those five words ("I tell you the truth..."), the completion of all of those sentences will contain important information about God. Would understanding and repeating those sentences to others be any way of testifying? The other gospel writers also include many "I tell you the truth..." quotes. Matthew has 29; Mark has 12; and Luke has 9. Combined, all of the gospels contain 76 "I tell you the truth..." quotes. For the Bible student, it is <u>must</u> reading!

<u>Chapter Twenty One.</u>

> **"You <u>must</u> follow me."**
> **John 21:22**

With the Resurrection of Jesus and his return to Heaven in the past, some of the disciples had returned to their former livelihoods of being fishermen. As they were out most of the night in the familiar Sea of Tiberias, Simon Peter, Thomas (called Didymus), Nathanael from Cana in Galilee, the sons of Zebedee, and two other disciples found their boat empty of any fish at dawn. They had caught nothing, but alas, from the sea shore Jesus called to them and told them to cast their net on the right side of the boat. Presto! The net was so full of fish they couldn't handle it. Wading ashore, a fire was burning with fish and bread already prepared for their breakfast meal.

I reflect back on the crowds of the 5,000 and 4,000 people that Jesus fed with a few fish and a few loaves of bread, and I think about these few disciples who labored during the night and caught nothing. How hungry and disappointed could they have been?

The meal being finished, Jesus talks directly with Simon Peter, son of John. Due to the three denials of Jesus by the disciple Peter, Jesus candidly asked him about his love: "Do you truly love me more than these? Do you truly love me? Do you love me?" Well, asking the same question three times in a row to Peter brought the same response from Peter: "You know that I love you!" It was a bitter_sweet reply for Peter to make in front of the other disciples; Peter was probably embarrassed by it all. Nonetheless, when Jesus reinstated Peter as one of the disciples, Peter still had some concern about the disciple John, and even questioned Jesus about him. This led Jesus to reply to Peter:

**"If I want him to remain alive until I return, what is that to you?
You must follow me."**

John 21:22

"Follow me," Jesus said. "Take your eyes off of other people and concentrate on me! I am the good shepherd; my sheep listen to my voice; I know them, and they follow me. I give them eternal life."

John 18:37. "You are a king, then! said Pilate. Jesus answered: "You are right in saying I am a king. In fact, for this reason I was born, and for this I came into the world, to testify to the truth. Everyone on the side of truth listens to me."

The Devil's Trap

[Paul's Letters to Timothy]

The Apostle Paul was a man of integrity and watchfulness. He was concerned about many things including people who would likewise become ambassadors of Christ. Realizing such positions were important, Paul outlined his thoughts about the character that each ambassador should possess, and along with that Paul would deliver words of warning, none of which was to be taken lightly. Paul was well aware of the wiles of Satan and how determined the foe would be to mislead and misdirect the followers of Jesus. Paul's two letters to Timothy contain valuable insight into this particular aspect.

1 Timothy 3:1 13

"Overseers and Deacons"

**He must also have a good reputation with outsiders,
so that he will not fall into disgrace and into the devil's trap.**

1 Tim. 3:7

The passage quoted above deals with Paul's observation as to the qualification of someone being an overseer or, as other versions of the Bible state it, a bishop. Anyway, it's an office with high standards and responsibility. The characteristics and duties of such an "overseer" are outlined in the first seven verses of chapter three. It is a position of leadership and importance. For the person desiring the office of deacon, verses eight through thirteen describe attributes that such a person should possess.

Among other things listed by Paul in his first letter to Timothy:

"He (the overseer) must not be a recent convert, or he may become conceited and fall under the same judgment as the devil."

1 Tim. 3:6

What is Paul making reference to in this verse, that a person becomes "conceited and faces the same judgment as the devil?" Do "recent converts" have a personal problem of pride similar to that of Lucifer before he became Satan, the devil? Would that then constitute the reason for judgment? It would have been nice had Paul been more forthright and precise to elaborate exactly what consisted of the devil's trap. He seems to be a bit vague about it in this his first letter to Timothy. Jumping ahead to Paul's second letter to Timothy may be beneficial.

"A Workman Approved by God"

The Lord's servant must not quarrel;
instead, he must be kind to everyone, able to teach, not resentful.
Those who oppose him he must gently instruct,
in hope that God will grant them repentance
leading them to a knowledge of the truth,
and that they will come to their senses and escape the trap of the devil,
who has taken them captive to do his will.

2Tim. 2:24_26

The passage quoted above is but three of the verses that are written in the letter of Second Timothy concerning this topic. The three verses above were quoted because they contained reference to the devil's trap. At this time it seems appropriate to elaborate on what comprises that trap. Paul does not detail much of anything concerning that issue in chapter two, but he does continue in chapters three, four and five to give information about the character of those living in the "terrible times of the last days." It is not a complimentary picture by any means! Paul paints a picture of people that lacks any comparison to that of Christ; he even cautions Timothy to "have nothing to do with them." And when he mentions teachers and those who have "itching ears," it all sounds pretty straight_forward, doesn't it?

The personality Paul proposes would certainly be desirable, not only for those seeking high office or as a representative of God, but just to have those traits as a common person in the community. After all, not everyone can be the leader. It is easy to understand, though, how quickly a person may become so engulfed in himself that he loses sight of God and, in essence, falls into the trap. For those who find themselves in this position, Paul hopes "that they will come to their senses!" This desirable act reminds one of the Prodigal Son who finally "came to his senses" while starving in the pig pen. (Luke 15:17). Take time to think and reason, especially with God!

Satan's efforts to deceive people with false information about God cannot be underestimated. He seeks to distort in any way possible the truth concerning God, and he will do whatever it takes to accomplish that task.

Satan is not in the world promoting himself and wanting people to worship him. All Satan has to do is misrepresent God and convince the religious community to worship the wrong picture of God. Has he been successful? Many religious people are more afraid of God than they are of the devil because they know God has more power than Satan, but they're not sure of the extent God will use that power. God is even accused of burning people in the flames of torment for all eternity. Who can trust a God like that?

When Paul says "and escape from the trap of the devil, who has taken them captive to do his will," (2 Tim.2:26) does "his will" refer to the devil's misrepresentation of God? How does anyone avoid being taken captive in this regard?

Since being tossed out of Heaven many years and centuries ago, Satan has had ample time to formulate a plan that seems so plausible on the outside, but on the inside the result of buying into the lies and falsehoods can be seen. It is plain to see where it all began in the Garden of Eden when God said "You will surely die," and the serpent's immediate reply was "You will not surely die." Who are you going to believe? Who's telling the truth? From God's statement of truth, Satan has blossomed that into the thought that "God is going to kill you!" And from that more misrepresentations occur.

Foremost and basic of all misrepresentations of God that the devil advocates is the premise that God, being a loving and just person, will punish the lost in the flames of torment, and it will never end. It is a loathsome picture of God, and many call that aspect God's justice. How can anyone love and trust a Deity who would do such a thing? Somehow Satan has corrupted the minds of religious individuals to believe his version of God's justice, and somehow it has been accepted as truth. Many other lies and falsehoods accompany this basic claim, but none seem so drastic in comparison. The devil's trap originated back in the days of Creation, and his seemingly realistic explanation appears to have embraced a large segment of followers ever since.

Paul wrote to the Thessalonians:

"Don't let any man deceive you in any way, for that day will not come until the rebellion occurs and the man of lawlessness is revealed, the man doomed for destruction. He will oppose and will exalt himself over everything that is called God or is worshiped, so that he sets himself up in God's temple, proclaiming himself to be God."

2 Thess. 2:3, 4

Who is able to oppose God, exalt himself over God, occupy God's temple, and claim to be God? One can only imagine the magnitude of Paul's description of 'the man of lawlessness,' and the insanity that such a person must possess to claim to be God. It is not without warning that we are left to contend with the lies of the devil. Paul continues to forewarn us:

"The coming of the lawless one will be in accordance with the work of Satan displayed in all kinds of counterfeit miracles, signs and wonders, and in every sort of evil that deceives those who are perishing. They perish because they refused to love the truth and so be saved. For this reason God sends them a powerful delusion so that they will believe the lie and so that all will be condemned who have not believed the truth but have delighted in wickedness."

2 Thess. 2:9_12

This passage by Paul was not written to frighten anyone about conditions in the religious arena in the coming days. It was written to convey the seriousness of the situation and the result of believing the lie instead of the truth. This all has to do with a person's belief system, and not a person's demonstrated behavior pattern. **It is in the mind where battles are fought, where truth and lies collide.** This, I believe, **is** the main focus that Paul is illustrating in this passage. The problem is knowing the difference between what is truth and what is the lie. The solution is attained by allowing Jesus to present that information to each person. As seen in this passage, the rejection of truth revealed by God will lead to the acceptance of the lie perpetrated by the workings of Satan. Those who are deceived will perish.

Paul does not leave us in a quandary or 'out on a limb' concerning this important issue. This is a battle ground where either truth or lies is the winner, and there is no middle ground or grey area that is okay. One will definitely triumph; the other will definitely lose. Accordingly, Paul writes:

"We ought always to thank God for you, brothers loved by the Lord, because from the beginning God chose you to be saved through the sanctifying work of the Spirit and through belief in the truth."

2 Thess. 2:13

Having expressed his gratitude, Paul concludes his message to the Thessalonians with the following words:

"May our Lord Jesus Christ himself and God our Father, who loved us and by his grace gave us eternal encouragement and good hope, encourage your hearts and strengthen you in every good deed and word."

2 Thess. 2:16, 17

"May the Lord direct your hearts into God's love and Christ's perseverance."

2 Thess. 3:5

Lastly, Paul admonishes everyone:

"And as for you brothers, <u>never tire of doing what is right</u>."

2 Thess. 3:13

Questionable Theology at the Foot of the Cross

The Death of Jesus.

1. Jesus, why do you have to die?
2. Jesus, who says you have to die?

Why is it so important that God's children, including all of the angels, understand what is happening At the Foot of the Cross? Is there a need to consider anything more than the shedding of Jesus' blood? What sorts of people are involved in the climax of Jesus' life on planet Earth? Is there no way the Cross could have been avoided?

From the accounts written in the Bible by various writers, the scene at Golgotha was not one of an ordinary crucifixion, but it was one of an extraordinary death sentence. Look around at the Foot of the Cross and see who it is that are rejecting God's Son, the One who was sent to represent the Father. Who is it that tells him his picture of God is false, that he is misrepresenting God? Who is being so cruel and expressing hatred? Who is condemning God's Son as a heretic? Who is accusing Jesus of doing away with the Law? Jesus came to explain everything, but they killed him rather than accept his explanation. Unless these important questions are answered in a manner that is logical and makes sense, it would be very easy to come up with wrong answers.

There are many who believe and think that God has said: "You do things my way, or justice requires that I put you to death, that I actually kill you! And if I want to torture you for an unending period of time, that is my prerogative and I'll certainly do so!" This picture of God promotes only one thing _ fear. How can anyone love a God who says: "If you don't love me, I'll torment you in the flames forever and ever, and it will never end?" What kind of God would do something like that? This is nothing but the devil's picture of God that the enemy of God has promoted since day one.

During the Dark Ages, martyrs were dying at the stake and were being burned to death. What were the priests holding out to them as they suffered in agony? The Bible and the cross! Here were martyrs being burned as heretics, and the religious community was the force behind this insane method of evangelism. Perhaps it could be said that this was a "heated" form of evangelism as it undoubtedly accelerated the thinking process of leading people to make a decision. Can you imagine the clergy being behind the torturing death of unbelievers, all the while holding out the Bible and the cross to them because that was the kind of God the clergy worshiped? The insanity of it all boggles the mind! Is modern evangelism any different than that of centuries ago? For those who travel all over this planet just to win just one person, are the clergy again using similar methods to evangelize the world?

"Woe to you, teachers of the law and Pharisees, you hypocrites! You travel over land and sea to win a single convert, and when he becomes one, you make him twice as much a son of hell as you are." Matt. 23:15.

Jesus, why do you have to die?

Can the answer to that question be stated in a simple explanation? Can simple words be used to provide the reason behind Jesus' death? Is it possible to look at the events of the Cross and come away with different views, all of which fit under a larger umbrella? And when doing so, would the importance of each separate view become less?

Unbelief and Opposition to Jesus' teaching about his Father.

"He was in the world, and though the world was made through him, the world did not recognize him. He came to that which was his own, but his own did not receive him." (John 1:10, 11).

Why didn't the world recognize and accept Jesus? Can the answer be found in the fact that the religious community had accepted and promoted the devil's picture of God for so many years, centuries, and generations that to deviate or turn away from that mindset would be tantamount to treason? Would leaving that form of religion and begin to listen to the Teacher from Heaven cause such a disturbance in the religious community that hatred and envy would entertain the thought of death _ Jesus' death?

"They hated me without reason." (John 15:25). Imagine! Insane religious people with the wrong picture of God!

Jesus' refusal to retract or denounce anything he said about the Father.

"Greater love has no one than this, that he lay down his life for his friends." (John 15:13).

How convinced and dedicated was Jesus to what he believed and taught about his Father? Would any of us "die" for what we believe to be truth? Would we be able to withstand the onslaught of verbal and physical abuse as Jesus did, and still be able to say at the end, "I forgive you?"

Jesus would rather die than tell a lie about his Father. It was the people who persecuted Jesus that spread the lies and untruths about him. Regardless, the threats and the emotional outbursts of false accusations had no effect on Jesus' mission to reveal his Father's character. Jesus' reluctance to allow dissention to alter his focus was evidence that he would never misrepresent his Father in any way.

Jesus' death reveals the character of God.

"Anyone who has seen me has seen the Father." (John 14:9).

The clearest demonstration of the Father's character can only be seen in Jesus. It was Jesus who represented the Father without fault. Whatever Jesus did, the Father would have done the same identical thing. Whatever Jesus said, the Father would have said the same thing. Whatever tone of voice Jesus used, the Father would have used the same identical tone. Had the Father come instead of the Son, everything would have been the same. The Father would likewise have been rejected, betrayed, and denied, and he also would have been crucified by the same insane religious people.

In actuality, Jesus' death per se does not reveal God's character; rather it is the way that God treats those who are putting Jesus to death that reveals his character. Does the Father bring fire down from Heaven and devour them? Does he utter words of rebuke from Heaven? Does the Father scare people with wind, earthquake, or fire? Is there a mysterious cloud hanging over the scene at the place of the Skull? Does a voice from above bring fear to those gathered at the Cross?

Jesus' death on the Cross proves that God does not want to kill people; the Cross proves that people want to kill God, and they succeeded in doing so. All of God's creation, starting with the realm of heavenly angels, the Universe, planet Earth and its inhabitants, everything God created says something about his character. Likewise, a benevolent and trustworthy God would not seek to destroy that which was a product of his creation. How strange that the created seek to destroy the Creator. How strange that today's religious community seeks Christ's blood in order to attain eternal life when eternal life is given as a gift to those willing to accept it. The story of the "Woman at the Well" in John chapter 4 verifies this. Jesus was more than willing to give her the gift of living water. All she had to do was ask for it!

Jesus, who says you have to die?

From the accounts of all four gospels, it is plainly recorded who is responsible for Jesus' death. The choice by the religious community between Jesus and a murderer named Barabbas was unanimous: set Barabbas free; crucify Jesus.

Matt. 27:20_22. But the chief priests and the elders persuaded the crowd to ask for Barabbas and to have Jesus executed. "Which of the two do you want me to release to you?" asked the governor. "Barabbas," they answered. "What shall I do, then, with Jesus who is called Christ?" Pilate asked. They all answered, "Crucify him!"

Mark 15:11_14. But the chief priests stirred up the crowd to have Pilate release Barabbas instead. "What shall I do, then, with the one you call the king of the Jews?" Pilate asked them. "Crucify him!" they shouted. "Why? What crime hath he committed" asked Pilate. But they shouted all the louder, "Crucify him!"

Luke 23:18_23. With one voice they cried out, "Away with this man! Release Barabbas to us!" (Barabbas had been thrown into prison for an insurrection in the city, and for murder). Wanting to release Jesus, Pilate appealed to them again. But they kept shouting, "Crucify him! Crucify him!" For the third time he spoke to them: "Why? What crime has this man committed? I have found no grounds for the death penalty. Therefore I will have him punished and then release him." But with loud shouts they insistently demanded that he be crucified, and their shouts prevailed.

John 19:14_16. It was the day of Preparation of Passover Week, about the sixth hour. "Here is your king," Pilate said to the Jews. But they shouted, "Take him away! Take him away! Crucify him!" "Shall I crucify your king?" Pilate asked. "We have no king but Caesar," the chief priests answered. Finally Pilate handed him over to them to be crucified.

The vote of approval concerning Jesus' death was accepted by the entire governing religious community that had gathered in Pilate's court. There was not one note of dissention to be found or heard while the drama of an insane trial took place. False witnesses, false testimony, and an overwhelming thirst for blood were the driving forces to put an end to Jesus' life. Rather than admit that their belief system was totally wrong, that they belonged to their father, the devil, the religious community was committed to silencing the One who told them they believed the lie.

John 8:44, 45. "You belong to your father, the devil, and you want to carry out your father's desire. He was a murderer from the beginning, not holding to the truth, for there is no truth in him. When he lies, he speaks his native language, for he is a liar and the father of lies. Yet because I tell the truth, you do not believe me!"

From the evidence recorded in Scripture, there is no doubt who is responsible for the death of Jesus. Influenced by the voice of the devil and totally convinced by his accusations and lies about God, the most religious people on the face of the Earth caved in to the devil's misrepresentation of God, the Creator. Their picture of God was contrary to that which Jesus demonstrated while living among his own people, and with certainty they rejected Jesus and his claims. At the time of the Crucifixion, the power of evil forces reached its climax. One can only wonder how such evil can continue to flourish in the religious community until Jesus returns because Satan's deceptions will continue to be overwhelming to the point of being unthinkable and unbelievable. Who will be able to discern and distinguish the false from the true?

Mirror, Mirror on the Wall...

It all started way back when...when angels first appeared on the scene. Created in perfect splendor and brilliance, they reflected their Creator. That first gathering must have been an awesome experience, and will probably, in my estimation, never be equaled or duplicated in quality again. Angels of perfection met with their Creator, and not a sound of discontent was found anywhere. What an atmosphere! Human beings can only imagine the magnitude of that assembly. But something happened that quickly changed the celebration. Peace, tranquility and satisfaction were being disrupted by one of the angels. The personality known as Lucifer was the first to notice something significant about himself. He admired his beauty, his physic, and his ability to convince himself about his own character. Lucifer had an "eye" problem in more ways than one.

First was the way he saw his own brilliant character as being comparable if not even more grandeur than that of his Creator. Also, the "looking glass reflection" told him his physic was far and above all other created angels. He was the 'shining star' that deserved the respect and commendation of all of the other angels. In short, Lucifer was stuck on himself. He had an "eye" problem as well as an "I" problem!

The prophet Isaiah says it accurately:
How you have fallen from heaven, O Morning star, son of the dawn! You have been cast down to the earth, you who have laid low the nations!

You said in your heart, "I will ascend to heaven; I will raise my throne above the stars of God; I will sit enthroned on the mount of assembly, on the utmost heights of the sacred mountain.

I will ascend above the tops of the clouds; I will make myself like the Most High."
Isaiah 14:12_14

Lucifer's "I will..." caused his exit from Heaven, as that kind of spoken language has no place in Heaven, nor does it have a place in planet Earth either. For any angel or any human being to claim to have abilities equal to our Creator is insane. If that was or could be the case, then there is and would be no need for God.

The "eye" Problem.

The pride of personal beauty and excellence proved to be Lucifer's downfall and down he went, from the courts of Heaven to planet Earth. Admiring himself while relying on his own achievements, and looking at himself in place of his Creator caused separation between God and Lucifer. Along with his angelic followers, Lucifer took up residence among the inhabitants of planet Earth, and his influence has progressed immensely since the days of the Garden of Eden.

Lucifer has sought to transfer his "eye" problem to the human race. Has he done a good job? I tend to believe so!

The "I" Problem

The "I" in the middle of two words identifies the human problem equally with the angelic problem:

L I E and S I N.

With the introduction of the "I" problem by Lucifer to the human race, the influence caused by it has not diminished over the period of hundreds and thousands of years. It can be readily seen in our world today how the intensity of telling a lie and of sinning have affected the human race and society as a whole. This is seen especially in the realm of the religious community where Jesus announced its presence and at the same time pronounced its effect. It was Satan, the devil, whom Jesus called **"a liar and the father of lies; he was a murderer from the beginning, not holding to the truth." John 8:44.**

Jesus is described in **Rev. 13:8** as **"the Lamb that was slain from the creation of the world."** What does that really mean? How could Jesus be slain at the beginning of time? Do the lies of Lucifer have anything to do with this slaying? Is it possible a person can be slain by words, words that lie about that person's character? Could this be how Lucifer convinced his followers to follow him and not follow Christ? Could his lies be the root cause of sin? Didn't Lucifer want to replace Jesus as Creator and insert himself on the throne of the Universe? Lucifer, of course, became Satan the devil, the one seeking to secure the minds of his followers with lies and falsehoods about God.

The Apostle Paul wrote these words:

"Don't let anyone deceive you in any way, for that day will not come until the rebellion occurs and the man of lawlessness is revealed, the man doomed to destruction. He will oppose and will exalt himself over everything that is called God or is worshiped, so that he sets himself up in God's temple, proclaiming himself to be God."

2 Thess. 2:3, 4

The extent of Satan's tactics cannot be over_emphasized. The deceiver will use every method at his disposal to portray God as the one to be afraid of, and at the same time make his own agenda seem plausible and correct. Satan's deceptions are not to **be** taken lightly as **they** are **"displayed in all kinds of counterfeit miracles, signs and wonders, and in every sort of evil that deceives those who are perishing. They perish because they refused to love the truth and so be saved. For this reason God sends them a powerful delusion so that they will believe <u>the lie</u> and so that all will be condemned who have not believed the truth but have delighted in wickedness."**

2 Thess. 2:9_12.

The above Biblical quote is powerful stuff. Imagine, the religious community delving into counterfeit miracles, signs and wonders, all kinds of evils, and rejecting truth, and because of that, God sends the delusion so that the lie is believed in place of the truth. What is the lie? Is it the same one told to Adam and Eve in the Garden by the serpent: "You will not surely die?" What is the truth? Is what God said: "When you eat of it, you will surely die" the truth?

Question:

Is it possible that the "I" has found its way into parts of today's religious communities, that it can be readily seen with the "eye? What would be its claims that all could see? Would counterfeit miracles, signs and wonders be visible? Would the claims made by those religious communities be acclaimed as authentic statements from God and authorized by him?

The Claims of "I":

> **I've been saved!**
> **I know I've been born again!**
> **I know that when I die I'm going to Heaven!**
> **I know that Grandma and Grandpa are in Heaven with the Lord!**
> **I can read my own heart and I can read the hearts of others!**
> **I know that I will live eternally with God!**
> **I know that those not in Heaven will live in the flames of hell for all eternity!**

Do the above statements concerning "I" take the place of God? Do they eliminate the need for God? Are these statements or similar claims repeated over and over by people who outwardly profess their spiritual condition? Are these claims any different than those found in Isaiah 14 quoted above?

Assurance of Salvation.

What ideal assurance would assure you of your own personal salvation? What kind of assurance that God could send from Heaven would lead you to say: "Good! I have peace at last; I know I will be saved!"

1. An envelope arrives in the mail box with your name on it. Inside the short note reads: "You will be saved!" Signed, God.
2. While lying in bed tonight, a voice from Heaven says: "You will be saved!"
3. An unexpected but timely call on your cellular phone from God says: "You will be saved!"
4. From out of nowhere an email arrives on your computer. You open it, and the words. "You will be saved!" are written in it.
5. Studying in your home, a piece of paper floats down directly from Heaven with your name on it. "You will be saved!"

Within today's religious community there seems to be an abundance of "I've been saved" people who are more than willing to expound their belief that they have "been saved" upon anyone who will listen to them. It almost comes to the point that they are bragging about their perceived condition, and even though they are sincere about that condition and are even willing to share their method of attaining that condition with others, it all is still just a claim on their part. Being able to read your own heart and/or the hearts of others is not within the capability of human beings. Better to leave that knowledge to the One who knows us all better than we think we know ourselves _ God.

Should our assurance be that only God knows the true intent of our hearts? As much as we want to think highly of ourselves and highly of friends, acquaintances, and loved ones in regard to their spiritual condition, we would surely arrive at a biased conclusion that has no means to provide substantial evidence to back up the claim. Reading the true intentions and thoughts of the heart belongs to God, and it is he, and not us, who has that knowledge to know so, and it is also his responsibility to do so. He alone knows the heart. All he asks is that we trust him that he does know.

For the person who believes he can read his own heart, could that be the spirit of anti_Christ? Is the person who usurps God's authority and claims to have the same ability as God the one that Paul writes about _ the man of lawlessness? It is repeated again at this time to provide added emphasis:

"Don't let anyone deceive you in any way, for that day will not come until the rebellion occurs and the man of lawlessness is revealed, the man doomed to destruction. He will oppose and will exalt himself over everything that is called God or is worshiped, so that he sets himself up in God's temple, proclaiming himself to be God."
                                                                              2 Thess. 2:3, 4

Perhaps the old adage: "A man is his own worst enemy" applies to this situation. In our own eyes we may perceive ourselves and others as worthy of being in God's presence for all eternity, but in so doing we have relied on a biased opinion of ourselves and others. If we think we have done all the necessary acts of kindness to others, that we have witnessed to others for God, that we have completed the criteria for sainthood, that we have manifested a spirit of generosity and selflessness, that we have attained a status with God that is pleasing to him, that we have reached the top of the mountain and are complete; if that is the case, we had better realize our folly and place ourselves in the hands of an all_knowing God who asks us to trust him. Always remember Peter! God knows our true character, and as much as we try to demonstrate to him our own "goodness," if we conclude that we have been "saved," that we've been 'born again," we have opted out for the unrealistic and the impossible instead by doing so. In essence, we've bought into Satan's itinerary. In place of that, forget about our own intelligence and trusting in our own personal beliefs about self. Trust in God's ability and knowledge about each of us instead.

Who Killed Jesus?

[Who's responsible for his death?]

It's hard to fathom and even more difficult to believe that there are those in the present religious community of Christianity who have attained notoriety and respect as scholars, who advocate in answer to the question **Who Killed Jesus? _ God did!** This particular belief is centered on **Isaiah 53:4** which reads: **"Surely he took up our infirmities and carried our sorrows, yet we considered him stricken by God, smitten by him, and afflicted."** That particular belief also cites the verse found in **Matthew 27:46** which reads: **(Jesus speaking)** "My God, my God, why have you forsaken me?"

My question: Do you, the reader of this book, agree with the answer that God killed his own Son? And if you disagree with that answer, what is your answer to that question? Hopefully, you have discovered the correct response through Biblical evidence. It seems logical to believe that if God killed his own Son, then neither humanity nor Satan the devil is responsible for Jesus' death in any way. This reasoning boggles the mind!

Perhaps to some people, the correct answer to the question **Who killed Jesus?** is mostly irrelevant. All that matters is the fact that Jesus did die, because **"without the shedding of blood there is no forgiveness" (Heb. 9:22),** implying Jesus' death on the Cross. To take this verse at face value then, one would have to say that until Jesus did die on the Cross, no person since the time of Adam and Eve has ever been forgiven by our heavenly Father for any kind of sin or transgression. And from that reasoning then, could it be assumed also that it was not necessary for anyone created in the image of God to forgive someone else? Does this seem logical? Let's see:

Adam and Eve ate the apple and disobeyed God, but no forgiveness from God. Adam blamed Eve; Eve blamed the serpent, and no forgiveness to be found anywhere. What a scene in the Garden!

Cain killed Able, and even though his blood cried out to God from the ground, there was no forgiveness from God. No need for Cain to feel guilty!

The Earth during the days of Noah before the Flood was full of violence, but no forgiveness from God, and God let everyone know that he was in charge!

The Tower of Babel brought about a confused language from God, but there was no forgiveness from God. God must have patted himself on his back!

At the time of Abraham as the cities of Sodom and Gomorrah were destroyed, there was no forgiveness from God. He wiped them out, period!

Isaac and Ishmael had their brotherly problems, but no forgiveness from God, or from each brother. How could God favor Isaac the way he did?

Jacob stole Esau's blessing, but there was no forgiveness from God. How could God ignore Jacob's deceit, but still bless him with twelve sons?

Joseph made a mistake and shouldn't have forgiven his ten brothers since God had not forgiven anyone. Joseph should have let them starve to death!

Moses struck the rock with his staff instead of speaking to it, but there was no forgiveness from God. God should have let them all die of thirst!

David killed Goliath and many others, and he coveted his army general's wife, but there was no forgiveness from God. David must have made a mistake when he asked God for a new heart; he should have kept his old one!

Isaiah's experience with a live coal that touched his lips took away his guilt and sin. That should not have happened as Jesus had not yet died!

Jeremiah's basket of good figs should not have come about and God should not have given them a heart to know him, because Jesus hadn't died yet. They deserved nothing but captivity and God's wrath!

Daniel should never have been able to understand visions and dreams because that would show favoritism from God, that God actually liked him. Another big mistake on God's part because Jesus hadn't died yet!

In more recent times when Jesus was "making God known" during his ministry on Earth, the following are examples of God's forgiveness before Jesus "shed his blood." The implication is, of course, that Jesus implemented forgiveness for a length of time before his death on the Cross.

Matthew 6:9_15. The Lord's Prayer. "...For if you forgive men when they sin against you, your heavenly Father will also forgive you. But if you do not forgive men their sins, your Father will not forgive your sins."(vs.15, 16).

Mark 2:3_12. The paralytic man. When Jesus saw their faith, he said to the paralytic, "Son, your sins are forgiven."

Mark 11:20_25. The withered fig tree. "And when you stand praying, if you hold anything against anyone, forgive him, so that your Father in heaven may forgive you your sins."

Luke 7:36_50. Jesus anointed by a sinful woman. Then Jesus said to her, "Your sins are forgiven."

It seems highly unlikely and improbable that the reference statement made in Hebrews can be taken in the context that Jesus advocated there was no forgiveness until he died on the Cross. It surely doesn't fit his character because Jesus and God are both forgiveness personified. This is validated with Jesus' closing statement on the Cross: "I forgive the lot of you!" To think that Jesus and God's eternal character did not include forgiveness until the Cross is ludicrous. They are the same yesterday, today, and forever. They change not! It implies that Jesus is saying while dying:

"Okay, I'm going to start forgiving people now. I've not done it previously, but now seems like as good a time as any to begin!"

What does the statement in Hebrews 9:22 refer to then? The reader is encouraged to read the entire chapter of Hebrews 9, as well as chapters 8 & 10. Also, keep in mind who the Hebrew people are, their ancestry and historical significance, and their familiarity with the ceremonial system and laws which pertain to it. The book of Hebrews culminates with chapter Eleven, (The Faith Chapter), and with chapters Twelve and Thirteen. For those interested in additional information on chapter Twelve, the reader is encouraged to read the chapter entitled: Hebrews, Chapter 12 found elsewhere in this book.

**Surely he took up our infirmities and carried our sorrows,
yet we considered him stricken by God, smitten by him, and afflicted.**
Isaiah 53:4

"...we considered him stricken by God, smitten by him..."

Question: Was Jesus really "smitten by God," his Father?

When we "thought," when we "esteemed," when we "considered" him smitten by God, does that mean Jesus actually was "smitten by God?" Is it possible that verse could mean "we esteemed him smitten by God" (but we were wrong!). Or possibly "we considered him smitten by God" (but such was not the case!). Or "we thought he was smitten by God" (but we were mistaken!).

In our everyday lives, how often do we go about from time to time thinking various thoughts about someone else, and only later discover that such fact was not true? How many times have we learned to our later embarrassment that the opinion we held of someone else was far from the actual facts? And then, when we are confronted head to head with those people, why are we so reluctant to rectify and set the record straight? Is this our human nature that emerges and refuses to admit wrong, and then continues on the same path regardless? It seems as though something needs to happen in our lives that would make us change course and head in a different direction.

My God, my God, why have you forsaken me?
Matt. 27:46

"...why have you forsaken me?"

Question: Was Jesus really forsaken by his Father while on the Cross?

Jesus did ask his Father that question while nailed to the Cross, but does that mean the Father had done so? Haven't you ever felt at one time or another that God and perhaps other people also, have forsaken you? David quotes in Psalm 22:1 those same words. Did God really forsake David? Does God really forsake us? In Deut. 31:6, Moses said to Joshua these words: "...the Lord your

God goes with you; he will never leave you nor forsake you." The writer of **Hebrews 13:5** states the same words: **"...God has said: 'Never will I leave you; never will I forsake you'."** This same chapter in Hebrews states: **"Jesus Christ is the same yesterday, and today and forever."**

I believe God forsakes no one, including Lucifer, the archangel who became Satan, the devil. God allows everyone (angels as well as men) the freedom of choice, and if we consider ourselves abandoned and/or forsaken due to that choice, it is because we have been given the privilege to do what we want to do, and in return we endure the consequence of that choice.

Who's responsible for Jesus' death?
If God the Father did not kill his own Son, then who did?
Is there clear scriptural evidence to be found?

The book of John records several instances of Jesus' own words as to who is responsible for his death. According to Jesus' own testimony, the evidence leaves little doubt who plotted his death and their reasoning behind it. In all actuality, the plot to kill Jesus first burned in the hearts of the Jews when Jesus first journeyed to the Temple just prior to the Jewish Passover, as it was there that Jesus encountered the money changers and the livestock inside the Temple. While showing disgust for the Temple being a haven for animals and illicit buying and selling, Jesus became an immediate target for retaliation because he was doing and saying things that were not kosher. This created opposition in the minds of the Jews. Nonetheless, it was first things first for Jesus, and physically cleaning the Temple was a priority (John 2:13_25). As can be seen later as Jesus deals with the Jews, physical cleaning was only one part of the cleaning that needed to be done.

1. **John 5:16 18, So, because Jesus was doing these things on the Sabbath, the Jews persecuted him. Jesus said to them, "My Father is always at his work to this very day, and I, too, am working." For this reason the Jews tried all the harder to kill him; not only was he breaking the Sabbath, but he was even calling God his own Father, making himself equal with God.**

Hard to believe, isn't it? A man laying on a mat by the Pool of Bethesda in Jerusalem, who had been an invalid for thirty_eight years, was healed of his disabling condition. He was told by Jesus to pick up his mat and walk, but the Jews renounced the man by saying: **"It is the Sabbath; the law forbids you to carry your mat." (vs.10).** Did Jesus break the Sabbath commandment by instructing the invalid to pick up his mat and walk on the Sabbath in full view of everyone? At least those who assumed they knew what breaking the law meant were convinced that Jesus had performed a "no_no" on the Sabbath. An act of this nature was cause for great concern by the Jews, as any man whose actions included this on the Sabbath surely had committed open sin. There could be no doubt as to his flagrant violation of the Law.

Can't you just visualize the Jews being so upset with Jesus, and then see how Jesus handles the situation in the remaining verses of chapter five? Within the verses of 19_30, Jesus states three times "I tell you the truth." The first is in **verse 19: "I tell you the truth,** the Son can do nothing by himself; he can do only what he sees his Father doing." **Verse 24: "I tell you the truth,** whoever hears my word and believes him who sent me has eternal life and will not be condemned; he has crossed over from death to life." **Verse 25: "I tell you the truth,** a time is coming and has now come when the dead will hear the voice of the Son of God and those who hear will live." Sadly, these three "truths" fell on deaf ears, which, coupled with closed minds, proved to be fatal flaws to the Jews. Refusal to listen and unable to discern truth results in bad attitudes.

John, chapter 5, contains a lengthy discussion/explanation/revelation by Jesus in verses 16_46. Intended to illustrate the relationship of the Father and the Son, and the importance of what happens between them, Jesus explains in terms for everyone to discern and contemplate. At the same time Jesus makes the Jews aware of their present incorrect beliefs which need some adjustment.

2. **John 7:19, 20. (Jesus speaking). "Has not Moses given you the law? Yet not one of you keeps the law. Why are you trying to kill me?" "You are demon_possessed," the crowd answered. "Who is trying to kill you?"**

Family political inclinations and pressure for public exposure, as well as the Jewish Feast of Tabernacles, set the stage for another confrontation with the crowd of Jewish people. This is the first instance where Jesus makes reference to hatred, as it is recorded in **verse 7: "The world cannot hate you, but it hates me because I testify that what it does is evil."** A question in point at this juncture might be: What is the evil that the world does? Could it be that the world refuses to listen to the "truths" that Jesus is telling them about his Father? Could it be that the world wants Jesus only for selfish reasons, to satisfy their physical hunger and thirst? Could it be that the world has bought into Satan's lies about God and refuses to believe the truth Jesus reveals?

Hatred can be like gangrene. Initially small and hardly noticeable, unattended gangrene will soon be in foil bloom and out of control, and later a lost cause. It eats away at the fabric of life and intelligence much like cancer, until the whole body and mind is consumed, and once that happens there is little that can be done to rectify the situation. Deep_seated resentment destroys relationships and makes any mutual understanding nearly impossible.

When Jesus asked the crowd why they were trying to kill him, their answer was one of denial, and they even went so far as to accuse Jesus of being demon_possessed. Were they unable to think clearly and evaluate their true condition? These people were still mad at Jesus for healing an invalid on the Sabbath, as verse 23 indicates. It's a bleak situation: people are unable to hear and understand what Jesus is saying, and at the same time they are loaded down with so much wrong information about God that they learned from previous generations. A reversal in the thought process needs to happen, and it can only come about through a different view of God, but if hatred is controlling a person's mind, failure to discern truth is not likely to happen.

3. **John 8:37 40. (Jesus speaking). "I know you are Abraham's descendants. Yet you are ready to kill me, because you have no room for my word. I am telling you what**

I have seen in the Father's presence, and you do what you have heard from your father." "Abraham is our father," they answered. **"If you were Abraham's children,"** said Jesus, **"then you would do the things Abraham did. As it is, you determined to kill me, a man who has told you the truth that I heard from God. Abraham did not do such things. You are doing the things your own father does."**

Historical name dropping! "Abraham is our father," they answered. Bragging that "Abraham is our father" doesn't cut any ice with Jesus. From Jesus' point of view, ancestral heritage means nothing, especially when that heritage is thought to have great advantage to following generations. Although Abraham was called the "father of the multitudes" and the "father of faithful," claiming him as their father is nothing more than a claim. It doesn't hold water!

The Jews who claimed Abraham as their father were told by Jesus such was not the case. Abraham was God's trusted friend and would certainly not plan to kill Jesus. At this point, it seems as though these Jews have a mindset far from reality. They don't understand how they could not be Abraham's descendants because of generational evidence and record keeping that proves otherwise. On top of this, it is beyond their comprehension when they are told they have a different father, especially since the person telling them has not been well received and has a questionable reputation.

Before Jesus was baptized in the River Jordan, John the Baptist delivered a message to the Pharisees and Sadducees: **"You brood of vipers! Who warned you to flee from the coming wrath? Produce fruit in keeping with repentance. And do not think you can say to yourselves, "We have Abraham as our father." I tell you that out of these stones God can raise up children for Abraham. (Matt, 3:9).** With such a stem warning given by John the Baptist before Jesus encountered the group of Jews in John chapter eight, there seems to be no change in attitude toward their heritage. Being a descendant of Abraham is all that matters to them!

Regardless, continuing the conversation recorded in **John 8:41 47**. **"We are not illegitimate children,"** they protested. **"The only Father we have is God himself." Jesus said to them, "If God were your Father, you would love me, for I came from God and now am here. I have not come on my own; but he sent me. Why is my language not clear to you? Because you are unable to hear what I say. You belong to your father, the devil, and want to carry out your father's desire. He was a murderer from the beginning, for there is no truth in him. When he lies, he speaks his native language, for he is a liar and the father of lies. Yet because I tell the truth, you do not believe me! Can any of you prove me guilty of sin? If I am telling the truth, why don't you believe me? He who belongs to God hears what God says. The reason you do not hear is that you do not belong to God."**

Make up your minds, people! First you claim Abraham is your father and then you claim God is your father. Which is it? It must have been a terrific shock when Jesus told them neither Abraham nor God was their father, and then to be told that Satan, the devil, was their father was just too much to take! Even though Jesus had performed miracles and many healings in their presence, being told they belonged to the devil brought out some strong criticizism toward Jesus.

With such feelings and emotion, **The Jews answered him, "Aren't we right in saying that you are a Samaritan and demon_possessed?" "I am not possessed by a demon," said Jesus, "but I honor my Father and you dishonor me. I am not seeking glory for myself; but there is one who seeks it, and he is the judge. I tell you the truth, if anyone keeps my word, he will never see death." (John 8:48_51.)**

Can't you just see the confident Jewish leaders now, knowing that Jesus had really goofed by what he had just said? The conversation continues: **At this the Jews exclaimed, "Now we know that you are demon_possessed! Abraham died and so did the prophets, yet you say that if anyone keeps your word, he will never taste death. Are you greater than our father Abraham? He died, and so did the prophets. Who do you think you are? Jesus replied, "If I glorify myself, my glory means nothing. My Father, whom you claim as your God, is the one who glorifies me. Though you do not know him, I know him. If I said I did not, I would be a liar like you, but I do know him and keep his word. Your father Abraham rejoiced to see my day; he saw it and was glad." John 8:52_56.**

Well, enough is enough! This man Jesus has told the Jews listening to him that neither Abraham nor God was their father, and that the devil was their father instead. Now this same Jesus, the son of Mary and Joseph, is telling them that he existed before father Abraham was born. They had heard quite enough from this imposter!

4. **John 8:57 59.** "You are not yet fifty years old," the Jews said to him, "and you have seen Abraham!" "I tell you the truth," Jesus answered, "before Abraham was born, I am!" At this, they picked up stones to stone him, but Jesus hid himself, slipping away from the temple grounds.**

Leaving the temple area, Jesus must have been terribly disappointed. He told them the truth, and their highly_charged emotional response was to use deadly force to rid themselves of this demon_possessed man. This was the first instance of threatening Jesus with death by stoning.

5. **John 10:31 33.** Again the Jews picked up stones to stone him, but Jesus said to them, "I have shown you many great miracles from the Father. For which of these do you stone me?" "We are not stoning you for any of these," replied the Jews, "but for blasphemy, because you, a mere man, claim to be God."**

Unbelief! Sandwiched between the first and second attempt by the Jews to stone Jesus are two episodes. The first concerns The Man Born Blind, followed by Jesus' explanation of The Shepherd and His Flock. It goes without saying that the situation between Jesus and those to whom he talks is deteriorating rapidly. Even more pointedly, Jesus is exposing their incorrect view of himself and his Father. He even tells those listening to him that they are blind, more so than the man born blind. Also included is the fact that they are not his sheep. No wonder the gathering of stones is quickly repeated! Unable to see their guilt of being spiritually blind on the one hand and not part of the flock on the other, the Jews are unable to think clearly as a group. **At these words the Jews were again divided. Many of them said, "He is demon_possessed and raving mad. Why listen to him?" But others said, "These are not the sayings of a man possessed by a demon. Can a demon open the eyes of the blind?" John 10:19 21.** Has Jesus made some headway? It appears at this point that at least there are some who are thinking for themselves and are not intimidated by others.

6. **John 11:45 53. Therefore many of the Jews who had come to visit Mary, and had seen what Jesus did, put their faith in him. But some of them went to the Pharisees and told them what Jesus had done. Then the chief priests and the Pharisees called a meeting of the Sanhedrin. "What are we accomplishing?" they asked. "Here is this man performing many miraculous signs. If we let him go on like this, everyone will believe in him, and then the Romans will come and take away both our place and our nation." Then one of them, named Caiaphas, who was high priest that year, spoke up, "You know nothing at all! You do not realize that it is better for one man to die for the people than that the whole nation perish." He did not say this on his own, but as high priest that year he prophesied that Jesus would die for the Jewish nation, and not only for that nation but also for the scattered children of God, to bring them together and make them one. So from that day on they plotted to take his life.**

Lazarus: Back from the dead! Four days in the tomb! And the Jews, the Pharisees and the priests once again plot to take Jesus' life. It was a shocker to those unbelievers when life entered the body of Mary and Martha's brother, and Lazarus came forth from the tomb. The inhabitants of the village of Bethany were amazed at this Jesus, and some of them put their faith in him. Others, though, tattle_tailed on Jesus to the Pharisees, who called for a group meeting at once. From this gathering it was determined that if Jesus was left unchecked in what he was doing, the Jews would lose their status and become slaves under Roman rule. There was only one option: kill the trouble_maker!

7. **John 12:9 12. Meanwhile a large crowd of Jews found out that Jesus was there and came, not only because of him but also to see Lazarus, whom he had raised from the dead. So the chief priests made plans to kill Lazarus as well, for on account of him many of the Jews were going over to Jesus and putting their faith in him.**

At the invitation of Jesus' three friends, Mary, Martha and Lazarus whom Jesus had just raised from the dead, Jesus finds himself in their company for a meal. The crowd of Jews found out about it and came to the house to see Jesus and Lazarus. This gathering upset the chief priests, enough so they planned to kill Lazarus as well. Why would the resurrection of Lazarus be so upsetting to the Jews? Was Lazarus proof of what happens after death that somehow was conflicting with Jewish belief? Somehow his resurrection by Jesus struck a nerve with the priests and everyone else involved, so it was decided that he too must die _ again! All of this occurred just shortly before Jesus' Triumphal Entry into Jerusalem.

8. **John 19:12 16. From then on, Pilate tried to set Jesus free, but the Jews kept shouting, "If you let this man go, you are no friend of Caesar. Anyone who claims to be a king opposes Caesar." When Pilate heard this, he brought Jesus out and sat down on the judge's seat at a place known as the Stone Pavement (which in Aramaic is Gabbatha). It was the day of Preparation of Passover Week, about the sixth hour. "Here is your king," Pilate said to the Jews. But they shouted. "Take him away! Take him away! Crucify him!" "Shall I crucify your king?" Pilate asked. "We have no king but Caesar," the chief priests answered. Finally, Pilate handed him over to them to be crucified.**

The threat of death to Jesus is over. Death now is becoming a reality. The words that Jesus spoke to the Jews in **John 8:44** ring loud and clear: **"You belong to your father, the devil, and you want to carry out your father's desire. He was a murderer from the beginning, not holding to the truth, for there is no truth in him. When he lies, he speaks his native language, for he is a liar and the father of lies."** It really hits home, doesn't it? According to Jesus, the devil is the father of these people and is also the father of lies. What a combination! A devil who lies and commits murder is their father. Could anything be worse?

Conclusion of evidence from John's gospel.

The gospel writer John has selected important information for his message about Jesus; about Jesus' Father, God; about the Jewish people; about the religious organization that includes the priests, the chief priests, the Sanhedrin. The Gospel of John makes it very clear that the people who refused to believe Jesus are the ones responsible for his death. The testimony of Pilate removes all doubt as to their knowledge of who it was they insisted be put to death. In the death of Jesus, sin has achieved its final goal. Along with this, the insanity of it all is clearly revealed, as those who are dependent on God for life scream for his death. May we never misunderstand who is responsible for the death of Jesus.

Also, the account recorded in the Book of Acts, written below, further emphasizes who is responsible for Jesus' death.

9. **Acts 3:13 15. (Peter speaking to the Men of Israel). "The God of Abraham, Isaac and Jacob, the God of our fathers, has glorified his servant Jesus. You handed him over to be killed, and you disowned him before Pilate, though he had decided to let him go. You disowned the Holy and Righteous One and asked that a murderer be released to you. You killed the author of life, but God raised him from the dead. We are witnesses of this."**

Lastly, from Matthew's gospel there is defining evidence as to who is responsible for Jesus' death.

10. <u>Matthew 17:22, 23</u>. When they (the disciples and Jesus) came together in Galilee, he (Jesus) said to them, "The Son of Man is going to be betrayed into the hands of men. They will kill him, and on the third day he will be raised to life." And the disciples were filled with grief.

**If God killed his own Son, it seems logical to say and believe
that the human race is exonerated from having anything to do with Jesus' death.**

The opening paragraph of this article contains the following statements:
<u>Who Killed Jesus?</u> _ <u>God did!</u>

**Surely he took up our infirmities and carried our sorrows,
yet we considered him stricken by God,
smitten by him, and afflicted.**
                                      Isaiah 53:4

For the reader of this book, this article concludes with some pertinent questions:

<u>Questions:</u>
How does a person even begin to accuse God of killing his own Son?
What does that say about the type of God that those people believe him to be?
How do people with that belief convince others to be God's friend?
Have these people really thought about what they consider to be true?

If the Father killed his only Son, does that make God a killer?
If God killed Jesus, can we, as human beings, wash our hands of any involvement?
If God killed Jesus, how does Satan, the devil, fit into the equation?
If God killed Jesus, could we ever trust him?

**God doesn't want to kill or destroy us.
Jesus' death proves that we want to kill God!**

**The Cross is the final evidence of what God is like.
God isn't killing people; people are killing God.**

<u>If God killed Jesus, what will he do to us</u>?

Figs and Twigs
"What do you see, Jeremiah?"

[Jeremiah 24]

"As the twig is bent, so grows the tree!"

<u>Hammers in the Fire</u>:
"Is not my word like fire," declares the Lord,
"and like a hammer that breaks a rock in pieces?"

Jer. 23:29

"The Lord your God is a consuming fire, a jealous God."

Deut. 4:24

The Figs.

Like any other tree that grows, the fig tree will grow in the direction it is bent at an early age. Left alone and without any outside sources to influence its growth pattern, under normal conditions any tree will fulfill its destiny by becoming an upright and healthy tree, but when certain circumstances happen to affect the growing, maturing tree, an abnormal plant may result. In the case of fruit bearing trees, the yearly by_product of that tree may be less than desired, _ it may even be called a disaster! The Parable of the Withered Fig Tree found in Mark 11 is no exception.

What did the prophet Jeremiah reply when God asked him "What do you see, Jeremiah?" He replied: "Figs. The good ones are very good, but the poor ones are so bad they cannot be eaten." One basket had very good figs, like those that ripen early; the other had very poor figs, so bad they could not be eaten. This episode happened at the time of the Seventy Years of Captivity, that time period when Israel was led captive by King Nebuchadnezzar to Babylon. For the "good figs" the Lord God will give them a heart to know him; for the "bad figs" the Lord God will send the sword, famine and the plague (or pestilence). It was not pretty being part of the latter bunch of "bad figs."

What brought about the Lord's displeasure? What preceded this division of the figs? The previous chapter of Jeremiah finds the prophet of God relaying a message from God to the people, and it is not a message of compliments. Rather, it is a message of concern that the people are once again straying from God and their leaders the prophets are at the head of the line beckoning them onward. Something is wrong, though, because the prophets are godless and they are telling the people lies as well as committing adultery at the same time. It's not a pretty picture as they fill the people with false hope and as they speak visions from their own minds, and not visions from the Lord. And the same prophets say, "I had a dream! I had a dream!" And the Lord said, "How long will this continue in the hearts of these lying prophets, who prophesy the delusions of their own minds?"

Tongue Waggers. False Dreams. Reckless Lies. The Lord continues, "Therefore, I am against the prophets who steal from one another words supposedly from me. Yes, I am against the prophets who wag their own tongues and yet declare, 'The Lord declares.' Indeed, I am against those who prophesy false dreams," declares the Lord. "They tell them and lead my people astray with their reckless lies, yet I did not send or appoint them. They do not benefit these people in the least," declares the Lord.

No one has listened! No one has paid attention!

Jer. 25:4

Jeremiah told the people, "Do not trust in deceptive words and say, 'This is the temple of the Lord, the temple of the Lord, the temple of the Lord'." Why would he say that to those people? Because "Look, you are trusting in deceptive words that are worthless." Jer. 7:4, 8. People, though, are stubborn, set in their own ways, and have their own beliefs about themselves. "We are safe!" they claim. "Safe to do all these detestable things?" asks Jeremiah.

"Modern_day prophets" are not few as one has only to stick around long enough to hear and see the same attributes that the prophets of old had that are picked up and carried along by similar men and women seen today. It's the same deceptive words, the same stuff: "I have a word from God; The Lord just told me to tell you; I have been saved; I have been born again; In a dream last night the Lord told me to tell you; This building is the house of God; We are safe and sound in this building!"

But it's Too Late!

Too late to realize their true position of being unable to hear God talking to them.

Too late to focus on what God wants to do for them.

Too late to recognize that the God of Heaven wants them to pay attention to what he says.

Too late to listen to God.

"Listen to me; Obey me, and I will be your God and you will be my people...that it may go well with you. But they did not listen or pay attention. Instead, they followed the stubborn inclinations of their evil hearts. They went backward and not forward."

Jer.7:23, 24.

And so,
"As the twig is bent from one generation to the next, so grows the tree!"

Motion Sickness in the Church
and
Deadly T.B. (Theological Baggage)

Routine! It seems as though nothing can match the ineffectiveness of any gathering of people for any type of occasion than for that meeting to be or become so structured that some kind of spontaneity is nowhere to be found. This is likely to be true especially in the realm of the religious community where weekly gatherings are so mandated by previous meetings that nothing new or different can be considered open for discussion. It's an atmosphere of sticking to the same method of doing things again and again, the same old way because it has worked so well in the past,... or has it? Unexciting and mundane are words that can describe such an atmosphere where the imagination and spontaneity of creative thinking are swept under the rug, never to be considered as a means to bring fresh life and vitality to an otherwise dull and unproductive program. The initiative to improve and improvise is often squelched at the outset of anything that might be considered radical and even ludicrous in nature. Why might that be? Could it be due to the fact that it is not in harmony with past perceived successes, and it's too much of a shock to change from the system that has provided stability and assurance for many years? For those who have provided the leadership and the bulk of the workforce within the walls of the religious institution, "changing the rules" is scary and mind_boggling as well as unheard of because it poses a definite threat to the security of the organization. It also creates an atmosphere of division among the constituents. This leads to a matter of toleration and whether those of the different views can work together and still be a cohesive force.

Ingrained thoughts that refuse to allow any new information to be processed in the brain are difficult to overcome. As mentioned above, it's scary to strike out in a new way when the past has been dominated and documented by success, at least in the eyes of those who conspire to maintain the status_quo and close their eyes and ears to anything considered different or new. To them, change is a radical word that presents uneasiness, and it's difficult to accept the unproven. The "sacred cows" are usually kept grazing in nearby pastures where they can be observed and maintained with relative ease. Why bring in "new livestock" to upset those already feeding on the traditionally grown grass?

Perhaps there is no perceived need to mow the grass or revive the watering hole, but it seems like moving on to greener pastures and digging a new well could have positive affects. Perhaps the old pasture needs to be replanted with new seedlings of grass, and the watering hole, instead of it being damned up to hold the same stagnant water, should be replaced with a stream of running water that is continually refreshing. It seems as though both aspects would be beneficial.

Who Is Your Father?

[John 8:1_59]

Teachers of the law and the Pharisees' Question:
"Teacher, this woman was caught in adultery. In the Law, Moses commanded us to stone such women. Now, what do you say?" (vs.4, 5).

Jesus' Reply:
Jesus bent down and started to write on the ground with his finger. "If any one of you is without sin, let him be the first to throw a stone at her." (vs.6_8).

Jesus' Questions to the woman:
"Woman, where are they? Has no one condemned you?" (v.10).

Woman's Reply:
"No one, sir," she said. (v.11).

Jesus' Closing Statement:
"Then neither do I condemn you. Go now and leave you life of sin." (v.11).

The Pharisees' Question:
"Where is your father?" (v.19).

Jesus' Reply:
"You do not know me or my Father. If you knew me you would know my Father also." (v.19).

The Jews' Question:
"Who are you?" (v.25).

Jesus' Reply:
"Just what I have been claiming all along." (v.25).

The Jews' Question:

"We are Abraham's descendants and have never been slaves of anyone. How can you say that we shall be set free?" (v.33).

Jesus' Reply:

"I tell you the truth, everyone who sins is a slave to sin." (v.34).

The Jews' Statements:

"Abraham is our Father." "The only Father we have is God himself." (v.39, 41).

Jesus' Reply:

"You belong to your father, the devil, and you want to carry out your father's desire. He was a murderer from the beginning, not holding to the truth, for there is no truth in him." (v.44).

Natural generational descent is the result of human beings producing offspring in their own image who, in turn, continually produce more offspring in their image. The lineage handed down through the generations grows in number by leaps and bounds as the multiplication of individuals escalates. From the union of two people, in a short span of time the number of sons and daughters, grandsons and granddaughters, and so forth, can be increased at an amazing and sometimes alarming rate. Take the number 2 and double it to 4, and then take 4 and double it to 8, and then take 8 and double it to 16. Keep doing this another 20 times, and the ever_increasing number is staggering! What has this to do with Jesus telling people who their father is? This example is used only to dramatize how, from one person (the father, for example), his descendants can become a huge, almost immeasurable number, and in the case of Abraham, how he became the yardstick whereby following descendants measured their worth and lineage. Abraham was the historical name to which Isaac and Jacob were the sons and grandsons, and those who followed after them considered themselves equally qualified to be called sons of Abraham. After all, Abraham (Abram) was initially called the 'father of the multitude,' but later was called 'father of the faithful,' and for those generations which followed later, they faithfully laid claim to their ancestral parenthood, and rightfully so! It was with high honor and great prestige to be called a descendant of father Abraham.

Abraham was chosen by the God of Heaven to be the initial parent of those who would represent God on Earth, that they would be the ones to demonstrate God's characteristics. It would be through this lineage of descendants that God would reveal himself as the God of the Universe, and he would do this by becoming an actual descendant of Abraham himself. And so, from father Abraham to King David there were 14 generations; from David to the Babylonian

Exile another 14 generations; and from the Babylonian Exile to the time of Jesus representing God on Earth another 14 generations. Count forty two generations in all, and the number of individuals in the millions! The final number is staggering!

Abraham was rightfully called "Friend of God" because he understood the importance of knowing the Creator of the Universe as he truly was. In short, God could trust Abraham with this knowledge because he knew Abraham's heart and his desire to know God. This relationship would prove to be the type of communion that God would desire with every individual, from the time of Abraham through the line of Abraham's descendants till the time of Christ's appearance, and from that time onward. The descendants of Abraham needed only to look to the example of their father Abraham to see and understand what God was all about.

But alas! As the generational gap widened from the time of Abraham onward, the picture of God that originated with father Abraham became distorted and muddled, and it soon became confused and later declared obsolete. Because of the distortion and incorrect information about God that was perpetrated by the devil himself, the decline of understanding Abraham's relationship with God increased and became progressively worse as time continued. In short, Abraham's followers became lost, and their connection with God became contaminated with error.

Upon the arrival of Christ, the longing for a deliverer that had been sought for many years became a reality, and it was Jesus who represented the last of the forty two generations from the time of father Abraham. Jesus was not only a generational son of Abraham through Mary and Joseph, but he was also the Father of Abraham, as he is the Father of all. The uniqueness of this seemingly impossible situation caused great concern when Jesus announced for all to hear that "before Abraham was born, I am!" (John 8:58). Such a statement coming from one of their own (a descendant of Abraham) was, at best, shocking, and for Jesus to claim that he and Abraham had previous contact and intimate conversation, that was the straw that broke the camel's back! In no way could Jesus be the Messiah, and there was no way that the descendant of Abraham would believe Jesus when he told them that their father was the devil himself Stones were gathered to do harm to Jesus, but he removed himself from their presence.

Historical name dropping (in this case. "Abraham is our father"), has little effect and does even less to influence a person's relationship with our Father in Heaven. That 'claim to fame' is meaningless in the eyes of God, especially when those who make the claim are ready and willing to do acts of violence that Abraham would never seek to do, primarily to kill God!

CHAPTER 24

The Cradle – The Cross
and
The Missing Dash

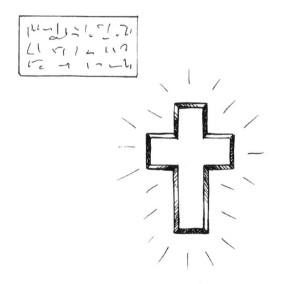

The Cradle – The Cross
and
The Missing Dash.

Christmas time brings with it the story of Christ's birth.
Emmanuel _ God with us!
Easter time brings with it the story of Christ's death.
Jesus, the Lamb of God, is slain!
Both are exciting times of the year for young and old alike,
whether or not any participation in church activities takes place;
whether or not the participants are dedicated church_goers;
whether or not formal worship takes place at that time;
whether or not the events are fully understood.

For some, Christmas and Easter are the only times when
that person's presence is noticed within church boundary walls.
These extra_special occasions seem to bring out the "good" in most everyone.
Planned services are sometimes practiced and rehearsed well in advance.
Most require much extra time_consuming effort in order
that the planned program is beneficial and successful.
The production of these programs is usually the two primary high_lights of the year.

With so much emphasis on these two events,
it appears to the Author of this book that
there is little time left to promote much else.
Hence, the title for this article.
Is it possible that The Dash between
Christ's Birth and Christ's Death is largely over_looked and
even down_played by the religious community today?

Jesus' Birth – Jesus' Death!
Somehow what Jesus said, what he came to reveal, and
what he demonstrated takes a back seat to the Christmas – Easter story.

To me, the Gospel is all of the Good News about God
that Jesus presented for all to see and experience, angels as well as men.
I believe the focus of our attention should be on the Father,
just as it was the main focal point for Jesus.
Our quest should be: To know God as he really is.
Jesus came to provide the evidence and what it means to know God.

The Birth.

It's hard to fathom that Jesus would leave his home in Heaven and become a human being like one of us. How is something like that possible? How could the Creator of the Universe stoop to such a level and still maintain authority over his vast enterprise? It seems as though he surely had to relinquish his power and his ability to govern all that comprises his entire creation. Is there a particular reason or purpose for him to go to such lengths, to even become an entity like those he created, to live among them, to share in their struggles as well as in their more pleasant times?

The Death.

It's mind_boggling to think that Jesus died on an earthly Cross at the hands of his own created beings, the people he called his own. The record states that Jesus was left alone and was even deserted by those closest to him. Death by crucifixion was no ordinary method of ending someone's life. It was purposely intended to inflict the greatest degree of pain and discomfort possible. No doubt it was excruciating as well as deplorable. Naked and exposed for all to see, nothing could be more down_grading. The amount of intense human suffering was intentionally extended and prolonged as long as possible. It was meant to be the cruelest of cruel methods of torture, and it successfully became just that.

The Missing Dash.

As mentioned previously, it seems that so much emphasis is placed on The Birth and The Death that Jesus' purpose and mission are largely overlooked. For instance, some people believe Jesus was "Born to Die." If that is the case, it seems as though Jesus went to a lot of trouble to accomplish that feat. Couldn't there have been an easier way than what he went through? Others believe that Jesus came to "bridge the gap" between an offended and angry God. This God could not and would not forgive his created beings until someone paid the price, and it was Jesus alone who could accomplish that feat.

Could it be that Jesus' Mission was to reveal what the Father was like, that Jesus came to "make his Father known?" This was necessary because people had the wrong picture of God, and they were actually afraid of him and his power. In order to relate to people on planet Earth and at the same time represent his Father in Heaven, Jesus became a human being and lived among those he created. His life during his last three and a half years was one of misunderstanding and turmoil. Even his inner circle of friends was often miffed by his actions and his conversations, and at the same time they were not confident even while in his presence to ask him questions. Perhaps they were intimidated and somewhat over_whelmed by the thought that this person whom they followed from town to town could actually be the person he claimed to be _ the Son of God!

Because Jesus was the exact representation of his Father, his qualification as such gave him authority that no one else possessed. Prophets, teachers of the law, high priests, and others who were part of the religious body of important people had a difficult time believing Jesus and what he had to say because he had not studied with them, nor had he received instruction from them. Jesus was an outcast, and an annoying outcast at that! He was a rebel who did not belong in the same company with the learned scholars, and he certainly had no business traveling around the country performing miracles, feeding the hungry, and offering hope and encouragement to those who would listen. And as a Jew, he befriended others with whom Jews did not associate, namely Samaritans. Jesus also was a friend of tax collectors, and he even was found in the company of prostitutes. His impartiality was a rebuke to everyone no matter what the class. Nonetheless, Jesus knew who he was and where he came from, and as such, he could remain steadfast to his mission of representing his Father. Nothing would sidetrack him from this venture.

The Gospel, the Good News, is all about God the Father. Is he someone to be afraid of due to his unlimited power? Should we tremble with fear when we envision him on his throne? Do we approach him on bended knee when in his presence and dare not to look into his face? Are we willing to do anything he would have us do and ask no questions? Do we feel intimidated by the thought of who he is and that we have no right to speak to him? Are we confident that he wants us to be comfortable with him and that there is no need to be afraid? Do we realize that the Father is as much our friend as Jesus is our friend, and if we are perfectly at ease with Jesus we can be perfectly at ease with the Father as well?

Jesus said: "If you've seen me, you've seen the Father" The old saying: "Like father, like son" is not limited to human beings, but it also applies to Jesus and his Father: "Like Father, like Son."

The Dash in between The Birth and The Death of Jesus has as its major theme the importance of "making known" God the Father. Starting especially with Jesus' ministry, the last three and a half years of his life fulfill his mission of representing his Father. It was not without consequence, though, that the completion of his mission ended in the manner that it did.

Instead of acceptance, rejection was found.
Instead of friendship, betrayal was found.
Instead of understanding, denial was found.
Instead of calling him a friend, a crown of thorns pierced his head.
Instead of a place in a person's heart, blood flowed down his face.
Instead of a "thank you" for a miracle, a slap across the cheek was felt.
Instead of acknowledging all the good that he provided, people spit in his face.

Regardless, Jesus' nature would not retaliate, nor would it condemn anyone. Even while dying on the Cross, Jesus could only utter the words "I forgive you," and know that if the Father had come instead of the Son, he, likewise, would have suffered the same death and would have said those same words.

There is a prevailing attitude within the present day religious community that God's justice needs to be satisfied in the end at the time of the judgment. This is thought to be a time of casting 'the lost,' the forces of evil, those enemies of God into the abyss or, as it is known by some, the bottomless pit. It is from there that eternal and everlasting torment will commence and where the gnashing of teeth will be seen and heard.

For some, it is a picture of a just God whose right and duty is to do so, but for others, that same picture depicts God as a revengeful tyrant "getting even."

For some, it is a picture of God's rightful indignation that is being fulfilled and poured out on those who deserve it, but for others, that same picture depicts God as one who has not an ounce of compassion.

There are those who see God as a loving, compassionate friend who was willing to correctly represent his Father, no matter what the cost. He was One who expressed patience and kindness as never before seen. This picture of God is quite different. This God has qualities of character that are not seen in normal circumstances and the every day run_of_the_mill. God is not someone who would humiliate someone else or distort another's character. He does not propose to torture 'the lost' for all eternity in the flames of hell, nor would he succumb to the notion of payback or revenge. He is not harsh, unforgiving, unreasonable, or demanding. God is a God of freedom who will go to great lengths to insure everyone's choice whether to accept him or reject him. He will never infringe upon an individual's right to make decisions on his own, and he will even die to protect everyone's privilege to make their own decisions.

Two thousand years ago the character of our Heavenly Father was expressed by His Son, Jesus. It was without precedence that Jesus' representation of his Father incurred the envy and hatred of his own people who were the most religious people on the face of the Earth. It seems as though Christ's journey on this planet met rejection at every corner. Why was it so easy to reject Someone who offered life, and why was it so difficult to accept as truth what Jesus said about his Father?

The Lord's Prayer

[John 17]

"Pray continually," the Apostle Paul admonishes the reader in 1 Thessalonians 1:17. The King James version of that Biblical verse reads: "Pray without ceasing." Such is the expression of encouragement that the writer of much of the New Testament evokes. The record of Jesus' three_year ministry accents prayer. One can read of specific instances where Jesus withdrew from crowds of people, and then could be found alone in heart to heart conversations with his Father. The Lord's Prayer that begins with the words "Our Father who art in heaven,..." is no exception.

The following article entitled "The Time Has Come" contains The Lord's Prayer, but not the same "Lord's Prayer" as mentioned above. This prayer is different. It has three parts: 1) Jesus Prays for Himself; 2) Jesus Prays for His Disciples; and 3) Jesus Prays for All Believers. Think about these three categories for a moment. Doesn't it seem as though Jesus is leaving some people out? Who are they and why would he do that? Does he do it on purpose? Is he prejudiced?

"The Time Has Come" is a lesson study of John 17 written by Dan J. Nelson. It is inserted in this book as a means that the reader may become better acquainted with the aspects of prayer as well as discovering the final revelation of Jesus' thoughts because it is shortly after this time period that Jesus is arrested and led away. The reader of this book would find it beneficial to participate with others and discuss with them when contemplating the answers to the questions in the study.

THE TIME HAS COME

John 17

It is fitting to find the last portion of Jesus' message to the world in the form of a prayer. It is in prayer where an individual expresses what they really want. The same is true for Jesus. In this closing prayer, we see his heart open to the Father. Here we find the goals expressed that Jesus has worked so hard for. We hear what he wants for his disciples. Most importantly, we hear what he wants for us.

What does Jesus want for you? It may surprise you, or even overwhelm you. It may seem impossible to believe, but it is true. There is no way to misunderstand the truth of this prayer, at least in terms of what Jesus wants for you. However, it is possible to ignore it, reject it or refuse to believe. Unfortunately, many have made these choices, but I pray that you will not. May this culmination of the Gospel Message touch your life with joy and peace.

As always, you can depend on the Holy Spirit to guide your thoughts in the understanding of truth.

Study John 17:1 5

Questions: What time is it in verse 1? How has this time been determined?

_____

_____

_____

What does Jesus expect to happen when he asks his Father to "glorify" him?

_____

_____

_____

Compare John 17:2 with 5:24 27. For what purpose has Jesus been granted authority?

_____

_____

_____

What does the giving of eternal life consist of in verse 3?

_____

_____

_____

What does Jesus claim in verse 4, and what connection does this have to the gift of eternal life?

_____

_____

_____

Compare verse 4 with verse 1. How are these verses related?

_____

_____

_____

Given Jesus' claim in verse 4, what implications does this have for the events which take place after his prayer?

_____

_____

_____

Study John 17:6 12.

Questions: Reread John 6:35_40. In what way, according to Jesus, has God been proved right in verse 6?

_____

_____

_____

Describe the act of obedience referred to at the end of verse 6.

_____

_____

_____

Because of their obedience, what takes place in verses 7 & 8?

_____

_____

_____

Does verse 8 describe the completion of the discipleship process? Explain.

_____

_____

_____

In verses 9_12, who does Jesus pray for and why does he pray for them?

_____

_____

_____

How has Jesus received glory from them in verse 10?

_____

_____

_____

How does Jesus ask his Father to protect the disciples in verse 11?

_____

_____

_____

What does this protect them from in verse 15?

_____

_____

_____

In verse 12 Jesus says that he protected them by this power. What do we see in Jesus that shows how this power works?

_____

_____

_____

Study John 17:13_19.

Questions: According to verse 13, Jesus wants the disciples to experience frill and complete joy. What is he telling them that will bring this about?

_____

_____

_____

Is Jesus referring to the same thing in verse 14 as he did in verse 13? I so, what causes such diverse reactions?

_____

_____

_____

Peace and joy are by_products of a life based on a love relationship with God. These are two feelings that Jesus wanted his disciples to have more than any other. Feelings which are impossible to have in an atmosphere dominated by hate. In fact, the nature of sin is to take away peace and joy. Selfishness cannot tolerate another life filled with these attributes, because it perceives that another individual has something it doesn't.

Are verse 15 and verse 17 just different expressions of the same request?

_____

_____

_____

What is the "word" that Jesus calls "truth" in verse 17?

_____

_____

_____

How does this truth "sanctify?" How does Jesus' example in verse 19 help us?

_____

_____

_____

Study John 17:20 23.

Who does Jesus include in his prayer in verse 20? What is his desire for them? Why?

_____

_____

_____

What is the "glory" given in verse 22 that leads to oneness? How can it bring such a diverse group of people together in this manner?

_____

_____

_____

Only when all eyes are focused on Jesus and the truth he reveals about his Father, will the uniqueness of each individual no longer present a problem.

Study John 17:24 26.

Questions: What desire does Jesus express in verse 24 for those who follow him?

_____

_____

_____

If this is God's desire, what can we expect from him today?

_____

_____

_____

In what two things does Jesus express confidence in in verse 25?

_____

_____

_____

What work will Jesus continue to perform in verse 26?

_____

_____

_____

Why will he do this?

_____

_____

_____

Fulfillment. Hope. Promise. Each one a part of this extraordinary prayer. We see the fulfillment of a completed task, as Jesus has passed on the gift of life to his followers. A gift which, surprisingly, is equal to their knowledge of God as revealed in Jesus.

We are filled with hope when Jesus prays about the reuniting of himself with his Father. We know that he has been accepted, that he has spoken the truth. A hope made more precious when we read of his desire that we be there with him.

Our confidence is bolstered by the promise of protection from God, of the continuing ministry of Jesus and from the confidence Jesus has placed in us by sending us into the world to finish the work that he began so successfully. May we never forget the essential ingredient to God's plan is the unity of Father, Jesus, Holy Spirit and believers in making the truth about God known.

Sticks and Stones

**Sticks and stones may break my bones,
but words can never hurt me!**

Not true! Totally false! The harm that sticks and stones can do is nothing compared to the amount of injury and discomfort that words inflict. Bruises, cuts, and abrasions can heal with the help of medication and surgery if necessary, but it's the harsh and vile words that, once spoken, are the real instigators that cause relationships to deteriorate and dissolve. Words spoken in haste often tend to be remembered much longer than any pain caused by physical abuse. It seems to me that before any sort of confrontation occurs in the physical sense, verbal accusations and abuse, as well as condemnation have always preceded such action, and the anguish and pain that they cause have no limit. Words can hurt.

Because communication between individuals generally begins with words, speaking to the other person involved is required. One person speaks while the other person listens. Then the roles are reversed. Conversation develops as a result, and as expressions are relayed from one person to the other, understanding of each other takes place. Unless one of the parties has an agenda to impress on the other party, an exchange of thoughts can be verbally expressed. Confrontation occurs when one party attempts to dominate the other party and control the situation. Blood pressures rise; the tone of voice becomes more forceful; patience becomes uncontrollable; volume of voice rises sharply; body language reveals uneasiness; facial expressions increase. It's not long before previous physical restraints are unleashed in an uncontrollable manner. The battle with the sticks and stones begins, precluded by the battle of words. It's an all_too_common experience.

One can only imagine the scene in Heaven as the first confrontation with words ensued. Can you see the drama develop as Lucifer, the arch_angel, presented his case before the throne of God? It was there that unkind words were first spoken by Lucifer, followed by more words that became pierced with accusations, untruths, and, ultimately, lies. Knowing it was futile to even think about using physical power to overcome God at this time, the deceiver was unrelenting in verbal abuse. Drawing sympathy from fellow angels, Lucifer embarked on a path to discredit the Creator of the Universe by pointing out God's perceived faults, and by doing so, elevate himself to a plateau of brilliance. Exciting the emotions and passions of other angels would enable Lucifer to promote his agenda: to take his rightful place of honor as creator of the Universe. His deceivable method worked splendidly as a third of the heavenly angels pledged their allegiance to him. His tactics of misrepresentation were well conceived and were carried out with precision, and once the ball started rolling, it gathered momentum quickly. It wasn't long before God initiated his plan to refute the accusations against him. Planet Earth was about to become a reality.

Picture the scene here on planet Earth as those who opposed Jesus during his ministry likewise used the words of confrontation as a means to oppose him. It seems as though whenever and wherever Jesus spoke about his Father he met opposition from the religious community, and no matter what Jesus said, there was a backlash of verbal abuse to be found. Rebuttal by those whom Jesus came expressly to teach was used extensively by those opposed to Jesus and his description of his Father. In relatively short order, though, rebuttal led to rebuke, to ridicule, to name calling, and eventually to threats of death. The slippery slope of degradation mushrooms and snowballs all at the same time. The scene quickly becomes unmanageable, and only the expulsion of the One who is thought to be causing the commotion can neutralize the situation and restore things in a fitting manner.

Before anyone arrives at the point of delivering physical abuse upon someone else, that person has made that decision in his mind. Initially, he may tell himself that the other person deserves it as payback for offending him previously. Actions just don't happen; they are the result of the mind at work, whether for good or for bad. Retribution doesn't just naturally follow insult, for example, but it is a common result of repayment for an injury incurred either physically or verbally. Deepening resentment is just a small step away from hatred, and when hatred is experienced in the mind of someone, there is no limit to the end result. With pressure building up, the release valve needs to be vented, and most likely the outcome will be violent. Events can become uncontrollable. One only had to look at the hatred expressed to Jesus to realize just how far thoughts in one's mind are capable of destruction. Physical action follows decisions of the mind.

In addition to verbal abuse and his eventual death on the Cross, Jesus was threatened with stoning twice. Death by stoning was practiced in times past as a means of ridding the community of unwanted people and animals as well. It was a cruel means of death where a large number of 'rock throwers' would eventually silence the person being targeted. The systematic and continual attack would be prolonged until the victim could stand no longer, whereupon additional rocks were placed on top of the burial site. It would stand as a grim reminder of the person and the event for which the person was stoned. I often wonder how Jesus avoided being stoned by the group of people who were in such close proximity to him. He somehow managed to slip away and was hardly noticed as he did so.

Is there a cure for the insane mindset filled with anger and hatred? Jesus told those who were in opposition to him that they hated him without reason, and that they wanted him removed permanently. Jesus was called 'demon_possessed' by some of his accusers who eventually called for his death as the only means to satisfy the insatiable hatred that had saturated their minds. Those people were experiencing total insanity, but they failed to recognize it as such. They could only press on to relieve the presence of ill feelings by eliminating the perceived cause of their uneasiness and stress.

Unbelief. What more could Jesus have done to convince those he came in contact with that they did not believe what he said? They likewise would not accept him as God's representative from Heaven. It's a losing battle when minds are closed and unable to objectively discern anything new or different than previous beliefs. It seems like a hopeless situation from Jesus' viewpoint. To perform miracles, heal the sick, feed the hungry, raise the dead, and still be thought of as having a devil, how could Jesus continue on, knowing full well the final outcome? He met ridicule and rejection most everywhere he went, and he avoided being stoned by those claiming to be followers of God himself. How frustrated he must have been, knowing what people thought of him and his Father, and how frustrated he must have been, knowing how powerful Satan's influence on a person's mind can be. But don't Jesus and God have more power than Satan? Of course they do, but when freedom of choice by individuals is the foundation of God's government, their power becomes subject to the individual. No one is forced to make decisions that are against his will.

Is it possible to crucify Someone with words as much as with sticks and stones?

FOTAP

[Fallacy Of The Assumed Premise]

Assumed Premise #1: Man is immortal.

**"You are either going to live eternally in Heaven with God,
or
you are going to spend eternity in the flames of torment
with the devil and his angels!"**

In other words, man is immortal and will somehow never cease to exist. The obvious question is, of course: What evidence in scripture states that man is immortal? The next obvious question is: Will God have to perform some kind of miracle to keep the inhabitants in the flames of torment alive for eternity so they can suffer for that length of time? The last obvious question: What kind of God would do something like that?

It started in the Garden of Eden when God warned Adam: **"You are free to eat from any tree in the garden; but you must not eat from the tree of the knowledge of good and evil, for when you eat of it you will surely die."** (Gen. 2:16, 17). Shortly thereafter, the serpent replied to Eve: **"You will not surely die, for God knows that when you eat of it your eyes will be open, and you will be like God, knowing good and evil."** (Gen. 3:4, 5).

Who are you going to believe: God or the serpent, the devil? God says "you <u>will</u> die," in other words you will not live forever. Contrary to that is the devil's version who says "you <u>will</u> <u>not</u> die," in other words you will live forever. Who's telling the truth? Who can be trusted? Accepting as truth the opening statements of **Assumed Premise #1** leads to the belief that man is immortal, and depending on whether a person is good or bad, he/she will exist for all eternity, whether in the courts of Heaven or in the flames reserved as eternal punishment for the wicked and the lost. And rest assured that the God of Heaven will see to it that the pain and suffering will never end. My question: How can anyone love and admire a God like that? It puts God in such a bad light.

Biblical Evidence pertaining to those who are mortal.

Gen. 6:3. Then the Lord said, "My Spirit will not contend with man forever, for he is mortal."

Job 4:17. "Can a mortal man be more righteous than his God? Can a man be more pure than he Maker?"

<u>Biblical Evidence pertaining to those who are immortal.</u>

1 Tim. 1:17. "Now to the King eternal, immortal, invisible, the only God, be honor and glory for ever and ever."

1 Tim. 6:15, 16. "...God, the blessed and only Ruler, the King of kings and Lord of lords, who alone is immortal and who lives in unapproachable light..."

<u>Conclusion</u>: Man is mortal. God alone is immortal.

<u>Assumed Premise #2</u>: Justice demands that God punish the wicked and the lost.

To satisfy his justice,
a loving God will "pour out his wrath" for an appropriate length of time
on the wicked and on the lost, whether angels or human beings,
and for that punishment to last as long as God shall live
is God's method of dealing with sin and evil.

My earlier published book entitled **Digging Ditches, Ph.D.** contains a chapter entitled **The Devil's Due [God "Getting Even."]**. Part of that chapter is copied below.

"...with liberty and justice for all."

Justice. It seems as though every offense committed against someone else has to be dealt with at one time or another, whether in a courtroom where legal standards have been established, or perhaps on a more personal basis where "an eye for an eye, and a tooth for a tooth" may rule as the appropriate method of settling an issue. If there is no offense, then justice is relegated to an inactive status, but, as sure as night turns to day and the Earth rotates on its axis from west to east, there will always be disputes that require some sort of agreement or settlement. And no matter what the cost, <u>justice</u> must be served; <u>justice</u> must prevail.

Will **God's justice** require him to punish rebellious people in the flames of torment for as long as God shall live? What kind of God would do something like that? Wasn't there a man named Hitler who loved to burn people to death? Is God like that? Perhaps God should be considered worse than Hitler because he's going to burn people for eternity! Is that what a loving God would do? God's wrath is not an act of punishment or retribution or revenge against those who choose to rebel against him. **God's wrath is:** he **will let people go...and they will die.** Jesus himself experienced God's wrath. "Why have you forsaken me? Why have you let me go?" are questions Jesus asked his Father as he hung on the Cross. Jesus was 'let go' by his Father,... and he died! In similar manner at the end, people will go their own way, and they will die, and God will be crying as they leave. God wants them to stay, but they choose otherwise. God offers everyone life, but compels no one to accept it. Everyone is at liberty to make up his own mind. The choice to leave God's presence, or to be "let go" by God, to be "left alone," is to die! All of these are examples of God's wrath.

Can you imagine God throwing people into the flames and burning them for all eternity?
That describes a mad, out_of_control, revengeful tyrant bent on getting even.
It's an insane picture of God. It's the devil's picture of God.
<u>That is not justice</u>, <u>that's injustice</u>!
And if people believe God to be that way,
how could he ever trust them to be part of his kingdom?

God's wrath is not punishment and torment for all eternity
as Satan and his followers would have us believe.
<u>God's wrath is</u>: <u>"he will let people go"</u>...and they will die the second death.

Stop! Look! Listen!

Stop believing the lies about God. Think for yourself!

Gen. 2:16, 17.

And the Lord God commanded the man, "You are free to eat from any tree in the garden; but you must not eat from the tree of the knowledge of good and evil, for when you eat of it you will surely die."

The #1 Lie.

"You will not surely die," the serpent said to the woman. "For God knows that when you eat of it your eyes will be opened, and you will be like God, knowing good and evil." Gen.3:4, 5.

God said: "you will surely die." The serpent said, "you will not surely die." The question is: Who's telling the truth? Did God tell the truth or did Satan in the form of a serpent tell the truth?

Did either Adam or Eve die when they ate the fruit as God said they would? No, neither Adam nor Eve died; in fact, nothing seemed to happen to them. Furthermore, they both lived many, many years after that episode. Hence, the beginning of the great controversy came into existence. Who were they to believe _ God, who it appeared was untruthful, or the serpent, who appeared to be correct? Besides, since the short time that had elapsed since Creation, nothing had died. No plants and no animals had experienced it. Death was something with which they were not acquainted.

Belief in this lie did not end in the Garden of Eden. A quick look at present_day organizations shows the same identical scenario, and this belief seems to transcend through much of the religious community, regardless of the smorgasbord of cultural and religious groups. There is no boundary to this particular belief, it seems, as it is part of the religious community world_wide.

In addition to this basic of all lies, Satan's influence to malign God's character has not diminished since Creation week, as his confusion and distortion of God's attributes have steadily increased with time.

Satan was a murderer from the beginning, not holding to the truth, for there is no truth in him. When he lies, he speaks his native language, for he is a liar and father of lies.
John 8:44

Stop eating the apple.
Stop internalizing the devil's lies about God!
Look at the evidence recorded in the Bible.

<u>John 1:29</u>.

The next day John saw Jesus coming toward him and said, "Look, the Lamb of God, who takes away the sin of the world."

Not once did John the Baptist point out to those within ear_shot of his voice who exactly Jesus was, but he did so twice (see John 1:36 also). This confirms Jesus as the one to whom John was the forerunner. Positive identification has been made as to who Jesus was, and recognition of Jesus as the only One who could 'take sin away' was made by John. A study of what 'the sin of the world' is that Jesus takes away and how Jesus does that would be beneficial to everyone as well as the reader of this book.

When we look at Jesus, who do we see? Do we not see God? Such was Jesus' dilemma when he was with the disciples. Thomas and Philip were not settled in their minds concerning Jesus and what he was all about _ they only wanted unquestionable evidence about the Father. Philip implored Jesus: "Lord, show us the Father and that will be enough for us." (John 14:8). Philip's request did not go unanswered very long, as Jesus replied to him: "Anyone who has seen me has seen the Father." (John 14:9).

<u>Mark 8:22 26</u>.

They came to Bethsaida, and some people brought a blind man and begged Jesus to touch him. He took the blind man by the hand and led him outside the village. When he had spit on the man's eyes and put his hands on him, Jesus asked, "Do you see anything?"

He looked up and said; "I see people; they look like trees walking around."

Once more Jesus put his hands on the man's eyes. Then his eyes were opened, his sight was restored, and he saw everything clearly. Jesus sent him home, saying, "Don't go into the village."

After Jesus placed his hands on the man's eyes the second time, the man "saw everything clearly." Did Jesus not do it good enough the first time? Did the man lack enough faith that Jesus could cure his problem? Why did it take two attempts for Jesus to restore this man's sight?

It seems a bit odd for Jesus to first take the man outside the village before he restored his sight, and then afterwards told the man not to return to the village. Why would Jesus do this?

Is it any different with people who are not handicapped or blind and have always had their eye_sight? Isn't it true of everyone that the learning process and understanding take time and that we usually don't get it right the first time around? Is this blind man's problem basically just a lack of understanding?

<u>Listen</u> to Jesus reveal his Father.

<u>Mark 7:31 37</u>.

Then Jesus left the vicinity of Tyre and went through Sidon, down to the Sea of Galilee and into the region of the Decapolis. There some people brought to him a man who was deaf and could hardly talk, and they begged him to place his hand on the man.

After he took him aside, away from the crowd, Jesus put his fingers into the man's ears. Then he spit and touched the man's tongue. He looked up to heaven and with a deep sigh said to him, "Ephphatha!" (which means, "Be opened!"). At this, the man's ears were opened, his tongue was loosened and he began to speak plainly.

Jesus commanded them not to tell anyone. But the more he did so, the more they kept talking about it. People were overwhelmed with amazement. "He has done everything well," they said. "He even makes the deaf hear and the mute speak."

Imagine being this 'man who was deaf and could hardly talk.' Your friends bring you to a person called Jesus and ask him to restore your ability to hear others speak. You are deaf and can hardly converse with anyone, and now in Jesus' presence you are not quite sure what to expect. Are you nervous and apprehensive? Are you uneasy concerning what is about to happen?

Jesus, of course, can read the man's emotions and his thoughts, so he immediately inserts his fingers into the man's ears, signifying what is about to happen to him _ the man's ears are about to be opened. Jesus then spits, meaning Jesus puts his own finger on his own tongue, and then touches the man's tongue, signifying the man will be able to speak. Jesus does all of this in advance as a means of letting the deaf and mute man know what was about to happen to him. Visualize this happening. Isn't it marvelous the way Jesus so carefully disengaged the man's apprehension before doing anything to him? With a simple spoken word meaning "Be opened," the man can at once hear with his ears and can speak with his tongue to the amazement of all of those present. The people had a correct assessment of Jesus, didn't they? "He has done everything well," they said. "He even makes the deaf hear and the mute speak." If the Father had come instead of Jesus, wouldn't the same identical thing have happened?

<u>John 18:37</u>.

"You are a king, then!" said Pilate. Jesus answered, "You are right in saying I am a king. In fact, for this reason I was born, and for this I came into the world, to testify to the truth. Everyone on the side of truth listens to me."

Admitting he was born to be a king, Jesus further announces for all to hear that he came into the world to tell us the truth about his Father, and to those who were willing to listen to him reveal his Father, Jesus would supply the necessary facts. Explaining and demonstrating the truth about God was Jesus' mission, and as he says while in Pilate's court for all to hear, **"Everyone on the side of truth listens to me."**

The climax to Jesus' life on Earth was about to take place. His representation of the Father was complete as well as his finished work that the Father gave him to do (see John 17:4). The disciples finally **"believed at last" (John 16:31)** what Jesus had taken three years to teach and instill in their minds:

"If you see me, you've seen the Father."

John 14:9

What more can a person do than extend the invitation for others to meet the One who is called the Messiah, the One who is known as Jesus?

**<u>The Invitation</u> by Philip to his brother Nathaniel:
"Come and see!" (John 1:46).**

Testimony

Human Personal Testimony (About Self).

"I've been saved!"
"I've been born again!"
"When I die, I know I'm going to heaven!"
"My name is written down in the Lamb's Book of Life!"

Jesus said: "You judge by human standards."
John 8:15

It would be better to leave personal testimony about self and decisions of the spiritual nature in God's hands. He's the only One who knows and can accurately read the heart.

Jesus said: "He who speaks on his own does so to gain honor for himself."
John 7:18

For those who promote their own testimony, remember Peter!

Peter replied, "Even if all fall away on account of you, I never will."
Peter declared, "Even if I have to die with you, I will never disown you." And all
the other disciples said the same.

Matt. 26:33, 35

Peter insisted emphatically, "Even if I have to die with you, I will never disown
you." And all the others said the same.

Mark 14:31

But he (Peter) replied, "Lord, I am ready to go with you to prison and to death."

Luke 22:33

Personal pride and confidence can lead a person to make all sorts of claims about himself, and especially in the realm of religious issues it often is the case that in order to validate one's presumed standing with God, a person may find out that he is not the kind of person he thought and believed himself to be. Such was the case with Peter and his acknowledgment that "I know myself!" As scripture records Jesus' predictions of Peter's denial and Peter's own words of personal testimony about self, scripture also records with accuracy the fulfillment of Peter's denial. And not only once did Peter deny Jesus, but three times he had opportunity to testify about Jesus. When the rooster crowed, Peter found out that he didn't know himself as well as he thought he did, but Jesus certainly did know him. Peter's bitter tears were the result of his not believing what Jesus said about him, as well as the fact that his own personal pride and confidence led him to assert qualities about himself that were not true.

Jesus' Testimony.

Did Jesus testify about himself? No! He testified about his heavenly Father.

"If I testify about myself, my testimony is not valid. There is another who testifies in my favor, and I know that his testimony about me is valid."

John 5:31

The Baptism of Jesus.

As soon as Jesus was baptized, he went up out of the water. At that moment heaven was opened, and he saw the Spirit of God descending on him like a dove and lighting on him. And a voice from heaven said, "This is my Son, whom I love; with him I am well pleased."

Matt. 3:16, 17

At that time Jesus came to Nazareth in Galilee and was baptized by John in the Jordan. As Jesus was coming up out of the water, he saw heaven being torn open and the Spirit descending on him like a dove. And a voice came from heaven: "You are my Son, whom I love; with you I am well pleased."

Mark 1:9_11

When all the people were being baptized, Jesus was baptized too. And as he was praying, heaven was opened and the Holy Spirit descended on him in bodily form like a dove. And a voice came from heaven: "You are my Son, whom I love; with you I am well pleased."

Luke 3:21, 22

The Transfiguration.

After six days Jesus took with him Peter, James and John the brother of James, and led them up a high mountain by themselves. There he was transfigured before them. His face shone like the sun, and his clothes became as white as the light. Just then there appeared before them Moses and Elijah, talking with Jesus. Peter said to Jesus, "Lord, it is good for us to be here. If you wish, I will put up three shelters _ one for you, one for Moses and one for Elijah. While he was still speaking, a bright cloud enveloped them, and a voice from the cloud said, "This is my Son, whom I love; with him I am well pleased. Listen to him!"

Matt. 17:1_5

After six days Jesus took Peter, James and John with him and led them up a high mountain, where they were all alone. There he was transfigured before them. His clothes became dazzling white, whiter than anyone in the world could bleach them. And there appeared before them Elijah and Moses, who were talking with Jesus. Peter said to Jesus, "Rabbi, it is good for us to be here. Let us put up three shelters _ one for you, one for Moses and one for Elijah. (He did not know what to say, they were so frightened.) Then a cloud appeared and enveloped them, and a voice came from the cloud: "This is my Son, whom I love. Listen to him!"

Mark 9:1_7

About eight days after Jesus said this, he took Peter, John and James with him and went up unto a mountain to pray. As he was praying, the appearance of his face changed, and his clothes became as bright as a flash of lightning. Two men, Moses and Elijah, appeared in glorious splendor, talking with Jesus. They spoke about his departure, which he was about to bring to fulfillment at Jerusalem. Peter and his companions were very awake, they saw his glory and the two men standing with him. As the men were leaving Jesus, Peter said to him. "Master, it is good for us to be here. Let us put up three shelters _ one for you, one for Moses and one for Elijah." (He did not know what he was saying.) While he was yet speaking, a cloud appeared and enveloped them, and they were afraid as they entered the cloud. A voice came from the cloud, saying, "This is my Son, whom I have chosen; listen to him."

Luke 9:28_35

We did not follow cleverly invented stories when we told you about the power and coming of our Lord Jesus Christ, but we were eyewitnesses of his majesty. For he received honor and glory from God the Father when the voice came to him from the Majestic Glory, saying, "This is my Son, whom I love; with him I am well pleased." We ourselves heard this voice that came from heaven when we were with him on the sacred mountain.

2 Peter 1:16_18

The Disciples and the crowd.

Then a voice came from heaven, "I have glorified it, and will glorify it again."

John 12:28

The life of Jesus is one of harmony and testimony concerning his heavenly Father. He did not come to attract others to himself; he came to draw others to God. He continually reminded individuals to remain focused on God and allow him to influence their minds with information about himself. Jesus pointed heavenward to his Father as the One who was to be worshiped and admired, the One through whom lasting and eternal friendship would originate. That example as demonstrated by Jesus is the pattern for everyone to copy. It is the pattern not centered on the claims about self, but centered on our heavenly Father with whom Jesus is equal. It is because of him we have the opportunity to testify not about ourselves, but about him. God is the reason we all exist, and for that reason alone we should offer praise and testimony.

Justice for the Persistent Widow
and
Finding Faith.

Then Jesus told his disciples a parable to show them that they should always pray and not give up. He said, "In a certain town there was a judge who neither feared God nor cared about men. And there was a widow in that town who kept coming to him with a plea, 'Grant me justice against my adversary.'

For some time he refused. But finally he said to himself, 'Even though I don't fear God or care about men, yet because this widow keeps bothering me, I will see that she gets justice, so that she won't eventually wear me out with her coming.'

And the Lord said, "Listen to what the unjust judge says. And will not God bring about justice for his chosen ones, who cry out to him day and night? Will he keep putting them off? I tell you, he will see that they get justice, and quickly. However, when the Son of Man comes, will he find faith on the earth?"

[Luke 18:1_8]

The plea of the persistent widow sounds familiar, doesn't it? "I have been taken advantage of by so_and_so. I am deserving of restitution for being treated the horrible way I was. I present my case to the court in order to receive that to which I am entitled." The judge, who has not an understanding of God and who cares even less for his fellow man, initially refused to listen to her case, but he now finds himself thinking of a plan to end her boring charade because he is just plain sick and tired of this widow being a permanent fixture in his courtroom. He only wants to be rid of her and her continual appearance in front of him. In short, she has worn him out! The judge would do most anything to quiet the complaining widow, and the only possible way to fix the situation from the judge's viewpoint was to give the widow, whether it was right or wrong, what she wanted: justice!

It seems a bit odd what Jesus says about the scenario above. The Lord said: **"Listen to what the unjust judge says." (v. 6).** Have we listened to what the judge has said for all to hear? In this parable Jesus calls the judge, who neither fears God nor cares about men, an unjust judge. Is he typical of most judges during that era 2,000 years ago? Is he typical of the present modern_day era? There seems to be no connection of compassion between the judge then and his fellow men. Do similar court officials appear that way today? The judge in the parable appears frustrated with the widow, and no doubt his patience, if he had any at all to begin with, has been worn dangerously thin by the widow's actions. It's time for him to put his authority of position into action, and not be bothered ever again with this court case. End it now! Serve notice that justice will be administered speedily!

The next two verses of this parable seem to make a slight twist as far as justice is concerned as Jesus now talks to his disciples about God's justice. Won't God provide the necessary justice on those he calls his own? Won't he supply the needed relief from the burden that his followers are experiencing? He is concerned, isn't he? How long will he not do what is needed? is a valid question. Why wait any longer? Jesus himself made the statement that **he will see that they get justice, and quickly."** That's the answer, isn't it? If Jesus' followers have problems that need to be settled in court, come to Jesus' courtroom and he will take care of proceedings pronto! But when and how does this actually happen? Jesus, no doubt, believes in justice, and he will be in charge of doling out the appropriate amount of justice for each particular case.

Be of good courage! Have faith, trust God, and believe in his judicial system. God's justice will definitely not be unjust like the one described in this scripture passage. His justice will be fair and the results will not be due to frustration and impatience as with the unjust judge. As Judge of the Universe, God will settle the issues at hand according to his nature, a nature of compassion and love, and he will not cave in to the impulses and demands of those in his courtroom seeking revenge. When that day arrives, God will provide the well_deserved justice as he pours out his wrath, and this wrath will be administered with the make_up of his character. It won't be a time of "getting even" for previously committed offenses, nor will it be a time of getting rid of evil, once and for all. Rather, it will be a time of quiet repose as the Creator of the Universe watches the final demonstration of freedom being played out before his eyes. He will "let them go," and people will endure the consequences of their own choices.

Jesus finished this parable with a profound statement which is actually a question: **"However, when the Son of Man comes, will he find faith on the earth?"** This seems to be a little out of place at first thought because what has finding faith on earth when Jesus returns, what has that to do with justice? What's the connection between the two?

In the previous chapter of Luke, the disciples requested Jesus to **"Increase our faith."** (**Luke 17:5**). In reply, Jesus told them in the next verse: ***"Go plant a mulberry tree, and I'll show you what can happen to it!"*** Actually, Jesus said: "If you have faith as small as a mustard seed, you can say to this mulberry tree, 'Be uprooted and planted in the sea,' and it will obey you." Wow! Mountains can be moved; mulberry trees can be cast into the seas! A tiny bit of faith can do great things! Amazing to say the least!

Faith in God; Trust in God; Belief in God. All seem to mean the same thing, don't they? When a person says he has faith in God, isn't he saying that he trusts God and that he believes what God says? There seems to be an endless number of Bible verses that could be quoted that relate to faith, among which would be:

> **"Without faith, it is impossible to please God." Heb. 11:6**
> **"The righteous will live by faith." Rom. 1:17.**
> **"We live by faith, not by sight." 2 Cor. 5:7**

But look what will happen previous to the time when Jesus returns to Earth, **"when the Son of Man comes: Will he find faith on the earth?"** Unbelievable! Preposterous! How could that be true? How could Jesus have a problem finding faith when he comes? Surely it could never be a situation like that! It's just not possible, ever! Why, our present generation is filled and over_ flowing with faith in Jesus and God...isn't it? Over and over, testimonials can be heard from people from all walks of life who declare their faith in God. It is no rare occasion when people state with certainty their beliefs in the powers that created the Universe and everything contained therein. How could Jesus not find faith when he comes?

The Healing of a Boy With a Demon.

When they came to the crowd, a man approached Jesus and knelt before him. "Lord, have mercy on my son," he said. "He has seizures and is suffering greatly. He often falls into the fire or into the water. I brought him to your disciples, but they could not heal him."

"O unbelieving and perverse generation," Jesus replied, "how long shall I stay with you? How long shall I put up with you? Bring the boy here to me." Jesus rebuked the demon, and it came out of the boy, and he was healed from that moment.

Then the disciples came to Jesus in private and asked, "Why couldn't we drive it out?"

He replied, "Because you have so little faith. I tell you the truth, if you have faith as small as a mustard seed you can say to this mountain, 'Move from here to there' and it will move. Nothing will be impossible for you."

Matt. 17:14_21

In Matthew's account of Jesus healing the boy with a demon, Jesus called that generation an **"unbelieving and perverse generation."** The King James Version of that verse states it as a **"faithless and perverse generation."** An unbelieving generation and a faithless generation mean the same thing: a generation that doesn't know God and doesn't trust God. Even when Jesus was on Earth 2,000 years ago, the faith problem existed. Was it worse then than it is now? The size of the mustard seed was mentioned then in Matthew and again in Luke as it would be in the day when Jesus comes again. Somehow faith failed to grow much before Jesus was on Earth, and it appears it hasn't grown much in the past twenty centuries either. What's going on? Why can't Jesus find faith when he returns?

Paul, the Apostle, wrote many years ago that "<u>some will abandon the faith and follow deceiving spirits and things taught by demons</u>." 1 Tim. 4:1. What are these things taught by demons? How could anyone be deceived by spirits that would cause them to abandon their faith? What could possibly take place within a person's mind and thought process that would eliminate the need for God to be part of his life in which to place his faith and trust? How could the presence of God not be an issue?

Confidence and pride in self and self's accomplishment are attributes that can reign out of control, especially when thought of in connection with God. It's the old **"eye" problem** over and over, again and again:

Like Lucifer, the morning star: <u>I</u> will ascend to heaven; <u>I</u> will raise my throne above the stars on God; <u>I</u> will ascend above the tops of the clouds; <u>I</u> will make myself like the Most High. (Isaiah 14:12_14).

Like Nebuchadnezzar in his hour of pride as he exclaimed: "Is this not the great Babylon <u>I</u> have built?" (Daniel 4:30).

Like over_confidant Peter: "Even if all fall away on account of you, <u>I</u> never will." (Matt. 26:33). "Even if <u>I</u> have to die with you, <u>I</u> will never disown you." And all the others said the same. (Mark 14:31). "<u>I</u> am ready to go with you to prison and to death. (Luke 22:33). "<u>I</u> will lay down my life for you." (John 13:37).

Like modern claims of self: <u>I</u>'ve been "born again." <u>I</u>'ve been "saved." <u>I</u>'ve given my heart to the Lord. <u>I</u> have arrived! <u>I</u> know Uncle Joe and Aunt Helen are in heaven with the Lord. <u>I</u> know that when <u>I</u> die <u>I</u>'m going to heaven! It's all about <u>me</u>, <u>me</u>, <u>me</u>!

What need is there for God when people proudly make claims of their own? <u>Why is there need to have faith in God, to trust God, to believe in God if a person believes he can accurately read his own heart?</u> Personal claims about self are like dead end streets _ no where to go! Where does God fit in the picture? Making personal claims of "I" have done this, or "I" have done that are meaningless to God because only God can read the true intentions of the heart. Better to leave that determination with God and trust him, and believe him, and have faith in him that he knows each of us better than we claim that we know ourselves. God is the issue at hand, not us. Our focus should be on God, not on ourselves.

So, for all of us, let's not abandon the faith, nor follow personal claims about self. Instead, let's remember what Jesus said to the disciples at the beginning of the Parable of the Persistent Widow. Do you remember what Jesus said? He said that they should **"always pray and not give up!"** **Don't give up the faith!**

"<u>Have faith in God</u>," not in yourself!
Mark 11:22

The Charge, The Confession, The Chatter.

[Paul's Charge to Timothy]

But you, man of God, **flee from all this**, and pursue righteousness, godliness, faith, love, endurance and gentleness. Fight the good fight of the faith. Take hold of the eternal life to which you were called when you made **your good confession** in the presence of many witnesses. In the sight of God, who gives life to everything, and of Christ Jesus, who while testifying before Pontius Pilate made **the good confession,** I **charge** you to keep **this command** (this charge) without spot or blame until the appearing of our Lord Jesus Christ, which God will bring about in his own time _ God, the blessed and only Ruler, the King of kings and Lord of lords, who alone is immortal and who lives in unapproachable light, whom no one has seen or can see. To him be honor and might forever. Amen.

Command (Charge) those who are rich in this present world not to be arrogant nor to put their hope in wealth, which is so uncertain, but to put their hope in God, who richly provides us with everything for our enjoyment. **Command (Charge)** them to do good, to be rich in good deeds, and to be generous and willing to share. In this way they will lay up treasure for themselves as a firm foundation for the coming age, so that they may take hold of the life that is truly life.

Timothy, guard what has been entrusted to your care. Turn away from **godless chatter** and the opposing ideas of what is falsely called knowledge, which some have professed and in so doing have wandered from the faith.

Grace be with you.

1 Timothy 6:11_21

From what does Paul want Timothy to flee?
What is the godless chatter he mentions?
The answer is found in verses 3 through 10 of that chapter, quoted below.

If anyone teaches false doctrines and does not agree to the sound instruction of our Lord Jesus Christ and to godly teaching, he is conceited and understands nothing. He has an unhealthy interest in controversies and quarrels about words that result in envy, strife, malicious talk, evil suspicions and constant friction between men of corrupt mind, who have been robbed of the truth and who think that godliness is a means to financial gain.

But godliness with contentment is great gain. For we brought nothing into the world, and we can take nothing out of it. But if we have food and clothing, we will be content with that. People who want to get rich fall into temptation and a trap and into many foolish and harmful desires that plunge men into ruin and destruction. For the love of money is a root of all kinds of evil. Some people, eager for money, have wandered from the faith and pierced themselves with many griefs.

1 Timothy 6:3_10

To Flee or Not To Flee!

The teaching of false doctrines and disagreement with Jesus' testimony about his Father implies that person knows nothing and understands the same. His unhealthy attitude and his erroneous belief that financial gain and status prove that God has been blessing him is wrong. Delving into controversies and arguments has left that person with an unstable mind, full of envy and hatred, and void of anything good.

Charges against Jesus
and
Jesus' Confessions.

As mentioned above in 1 Tim. 6:13 ("and of Christ Jesus, who while testifying before Pontius Pilate made the good confession"), those confessions along with the charges against Jesus as recorded in the four gospels are written below. Notice that Matthew, Mark, and Luke are very similar in recording the charges and the confessions, but the gospel of John has a different flavor to it. Why might that be? Did John hear and see it from a different angle? Did he have an advantage over the other three writers? It is interesting to note that Jesus' confession in Pilate's court, according to John, is loaded with Jesus' last testimony about his mission: to testify to the truth about God!

Matt. 26:63. The high priest's charge:
The high priest said to him: "I charge you under oath by the living God: Tell us if you are the Christ, the Son of God."

Matt. 26:64. Jesus' confession:
"Yes, it is as you say," Jesus replied. "But I say to all of you: In the future you will see the Son of Man sitting at the right hand of the Mighty One and coming on the clouds of heaven."

Matt. 27:11. Pilate's charge:
Meanwhile Jesus stood before the governor, and the governor asked him, "Are you the king of the Jews?"

Matt. 27:11. Jesus' confession:
"Yes, it is as you say," Jesus replied.

<u>Mark 14:61</u>. The high priest's charge:

Again the high priest asked him, "Are you the Christ, the Son of the Blessed One?"

<u>Mark 14:62</u>. Jesus' confession:

"I am," said Jesus. "And you will see the Son of Man sitting at the right hand of the Mighty One and coming on the clouds of heaven."

<u>Mark 15:2</u>. Pilate's charge:

"Are you the king of the Jews?" asked Pilate.

<u>Mark 15:2</u>. Jesus' confession:

"Yes, it is as you say," Jesus replied.

<u>Luke 22:67</u>. The chief priest and teacher's of the law charge:

"If you are the Christ," they said, "tell us."

<u>Luke 22:67</u>. Jesus' confession:

Jesus answered, "If I tell you, you will not believe me, and if I asked you, you would not answer. But from now on, the Son of Man will be seated at the right hand of the Mighty God."

<u>Luke 22:70</u>. The chief priest and teacher's of the law charge:

They all asked: "Are you then the Son of God?"

<u>Luke 22:70</u>. Jesus' confession:

He replied, "You are right in saying I am."

<u>Luke 23:3</u>. Pilate's charge:

So Pilate asked Jesus, "Are you the king of the Jews?"

<u>Luke 23:3</u>. Jesus' confession:

"Yes, it is as you say," Jesus replied.

<u>John 18:12 14</u>. Then the detachment of soldiers with its commander and the Jewish officials arrested Jesus. The bound him and brought him first to Annas, who was the father in law of Caiaphas, the high priest that year. Caiaphas was the one who advised the Jews that it would be good if one man died for the people.

<u>John 18:19 21</u>. Meanwhile, the high priest questioned Jesus about his disciples and his teaching. "I have spoken openly to the world," Jesus replied. "I always taught in synagogues or at the temple, where all the Jews come together. I said nothing in secret. Why question me? Ask those who heard me. Surely they know what I said."

<u>John 18:28</u>. Then the Jews led Jesus from Caiaphas to the palace of the Roman governor. By now it was early morning, and to avoid ceremonial uncleanness the Jews did not enter the palace; they wanted to be able to eat the Passover.

<u>John 18:33</u>. Pilate's charge:
  Pilate then went back inside the palace, summoned Jesus and asked him, "Are you the king of the Jews?"

<u>John 18:34</u>. Jesus' confession:
  "Is that your own idea," Jesus asked, "or did others talk to you about me?"

<u>John 18:37</u>. Pilate's charge:
  "You are a king, then!" said Pilate.

<u>John 18:37</u>. Jesus' confession:
  Jesus answered, "You are right in saying I am a king. In fact, for this reason I was born, and for this I came into the world, to testify to the truth. Everyone on the side of truth listens to me."

The last two verses quoted at the beginning of this article are written again for further consideration. Paul's concern for Timothy is vividly revealed in his choice of words written in response to the current situation at that time:

Timothy, guard what has been entrusted to your care. Turn away from <u>godless chatter</u> and the opposing ideas of what is falsely called knowledge, which some have professed and in so doing have wandered from the faith.

1 Tim. 6:20, 21

Whatever may be the case that causes a person to wander from the faith, Paul instructs Timothy to keep his distance from it. How would a person wander from the faith? What would **godless chatter** be comprised of and what is Paul talking about when he mentions false knowledge? Would any of this have to do with having the wrong picture of God? Would false knowledge involve the lies of the devil? Would any of this have to do with personal claims about self?

Paul's remarks to Timothy do not end with his first letter to Timothy. Paul's second letter to Timothy seems to continue in this same vein of thought, especially in Chapter 2:14_26, Chapter 3, and Chapter 4:1_5. Paul again mentions to Timothy about the **godless chatter** in chapter two, verse sixteen. The reader of this book is encouraged to read those thoughts written by Paul.

Eternal Life Given

Not many people want to die. Most everyone wants to live, and to live forever, eternally. It is most natural to have that concern not only for oneself, but for family, friends, and acquaintances who are loved and respected for the people they are. Anything short of attaining this eternal life means a separation between friendships.

Jesus prayed to his Father:
"Father, the time has come. Glorify your Son, that your Son may glorify you. For you granted him authority over all people that he might give eternal life to all those you have given him. Now this is eternal life: that they may know you, the only true God, and Jesus Christ, whom you have sent. I have brought you glory on earth by completing the work you gave me to do. And now, Father, glorify me in your presence with the glory I had with you before the world began."

John 17:1_5

Eternal Life = **Knowing God.** Eternal Life means receiving knowledge about God, the information revealed by Jesus his Son. This knowledge, this information concerning the Father, is being made known to us by the Son. It is a gift, and it is our choice whether to accept or reject that gift, that information.

John 4:10 14. Woman at the Well.

Jesus answered her, "If you knew the gift of God and who it is that asks you for a drink, you would have asked him and he would have given you living water."

"Sir," the woman said, "you have nothing to draw with and the well is deep. Where can you get this living water? Are you greater than our father Jacob, who gave us the well and drank from it himself, as did also his sons and flocks and herds?"

Jesus answered, "Everyone who drinks this water will be thirsty again, but whoever drinks the water I give him will never thirst. Indeed, the water I give him will become in him a spring of water welling up to eternal life."

John 5:21, 24 26.

"For just as the Father raises the dead and gives them life, even so the Son gives life to whom he is pleased to give it."

"I tell you the truth, whoever hears my word and believes him who sent me has eternal life and will not be condemned; he has crossed over from death to life. I tell you the truth, a time is coming and has now come when the dead will hear the voice of the Son of God and those who hear will live. For as the Father has life in himself, so he has granted the Son to have life in himself."

John 6:27, 33, 35, 40, 47, 48, 51, 54, 58, 63, 68.

"Do not work for food that spoils, but for food that endures to eternal life, which the Son of Man will give you. On him God the Father has placed his seal of approval."

"For the bread of God is he who comes down from heaven and gives life to the world."

Then Jesus declared, "I am the bread of life. He who comes to me will never go hungry and he who believes in me will never be thirsty."

"For my Father's will is that everyone who looks to the Son and believes in him shall have eternal life."

"I tell you the truth, he who believes has everlasting life."

"I am the bread of life."

"I am the living bread that came down from heaven. If anyone eats of this bread, he will live forever. This bread is my flesh, which I will give for the life of the world."

"Whosoever eats my flesh and drinks my blood has eternal life, and I will raise him up the last day."

"This is the bread that came down from heaven. Your forefathers ate manna and died, but he who feeds on this bread will live forever."

"The Spirit gives life; the flesh counts for nothing. The words I have spoken to you are spirit and they are life."

Simon Peter answered him, "Lord, to whom shall we go? You have the words of eternal life."

John 8:12.

When Jesus spoke again to the people, he said, "I am the light of the world. Whoever follows me will never walk in darkness, but will have the light of life."

John 10:10, 27, 28.

"The thief comes only to steal and kill and destroy; I have come that they may have life, and have it to the full."

"My sheep listen to my voice; I know them, and they follow me. I give them eternal life, and they shall never perish; no one can snatch them out of my hand."

John 11:25.

Jesus said to her, "I am the resurrection and the life. He who believes in me will live, even though he dies; and whoever lives and believes in me will never die. Do you believe this?"

John 12:49, 50.

"For I did not speak of my own accord, but the Father who sent me commanded me what to say and how to say it. I know that his command leads to eternal life. So whatever I say is just what the Father has told me to say."

John 14:6.

Jesus answered, "I am the way and the truth and the life. No one comes to the Father except through me."

Life! Eternal Life!

Rather than being the reward that people receive at the end of their earthly lifespan, and rather than being the reward received at the Second Coming of Christ, eternal life is the gift of knowledge and information given to us during this lifetime. Depending upon our acceptance or rejection of that information, our time spent in eternity with God will be determined. Jesus, God's Son, has "made known" his Father by revealing this knowledge and information about him, and he has left it up to us to decide whether we want to be part of his kingdom.

Eternal Life _ the Gospel, the Good News about God.

It's all about God; it's not about us! Is God the person that Jesus claimed and described him to be, or is he something contrary to that description? Is Jesus God's exact representative as the author of the book of Hebrews claims in chapter one, verse three? Is "making God known" Jesus' mission?

Eternal Life is not so much intended to be thought of as to its length of duration, but rather to the type and the quality of life that is being lived. There is much current belief and speculation about the existence of an eternal hell fire where 'the lost' will live forever in the flames of torment. Shouldn't this type of existence be called eternal life also? I mean, it is presumed that they will live in that condition forever. It makes no sense to me to believe that eternal suffering in the flames somehow satisfies God's need for justice. That picture does not present God as One who is loving and trustworthy. He becomes a fearful Deity, and One to be afraid of with all of that power.

John 20:30, 31.

Jesus did many other miraculous signs in the presence of his disciples, which are not recorded in this book. But these are written that you may believe that Jesus is the Christ, the Son of God, and that by believing you may have life in his name.

CHAPTER 33

Imagination is better than knowledge.

Albert Einstein

Can You Imagine?

Imagine yourself at a young age in a beginner's arithmetic class where you are being exposed to numbers. Your teacher is explaining to you and your classmates the value of numbers and how they relate to each other. If, by example and demonstration, your teacher told you that 2 + 2 = 4, would you believe him? In all probability, most students would agree with the teacher that 2 apples plus 2 apples equals 4 apples. Simple addition, right? It just makes sense that 2 + 2 = 4 because that fact is correct. To think that 2 + 2 = 3 is not right, neither is 2 + 2 = 5 correct. There is only one correct answer to this basic arithmetic problem. Imagine the futility to argue with the teacher about this equation. The point of all of this is that when a person believes certain facts presented by someone else, truth has been accepted into that person's belief system. It's right because it is right!

The Woman at the Well. [John 4:1_26].

Jesus encounters this Samaritan woman of dubious reputation at Jacob's well near the town of Sychar. Both appear to be in need of a drink of water as Jesus is a bit weary from the journey with his disciples and the woman is there at the well to refill her water jar for the day's supply. An amazing thing happens at this encounter. Jesus, a Jew, asks a woman who is a Samaritan for a drink of water. This is unheard of because the two nationalities do not associate or rely on each other for anything, and of even greater ambiguity is the fact that Jesus is a man asking this Samaritan woman for a drink. Things like this are not kosher to say the least.

Jesus is thirsty; the woman is thirsty, but little does she realize what Jesus knows about her. Jesus knows everything there is to know about her, and a lot of it is not very complimentary, but that does not deter him. Jesus offers this woman what she really needs to drink, and it's not water from Jacob's well. The water that Jesus offers will become a spring of water welling up to eternal life. The woman has been thinking all of her life about physical water to maintain life, and now someone is telling her news about a different kind of water, and she wants some of it.

Conversation continues between these two figures at the well until the disciples return from town with food. At that time the woman leaves everything she has (the water jar) and returns to town, telling everyone everything about a particular person she has just met. "Come, see a man who told me everything I ever did. Could this be the Christ?" she asks. Strange isn't it how a stranger could know the deep_down yearnings of another person's heart? The woman is not embarrassed by this knowledge that Jesus has of her; she only wants the town people to meet him! The woman is impressed with Jesus!

Samaritans Who Believe. [John 4:39_42].

This brief antidote to the Woman at the Well serves as added evidence to the thought that 'right is right because it is right.' The town people believe, not because of the woman's testimony but because they have figured it out for themselves that what Jesus told them was truth. It all added up! They became believers! They liked Jesus!

The Invalid at the Pool of Bethesda. [John 5:1_15].

For some individuals, thirty_eight years is not a long period of time, but for the man who was an invalid, it's a lifetime. Alone by the pool, the man needs assistance to enter the pool when the water is stirred, but no one will help him. Along comes Jesus who is willing to provide the cure which the man really needs. Initially, the man didn't know that it was Jesus who cured him, but he found out the truth later. The once_invalid man announced to the Jews that it was Jesus who had made him well.

Jesus Feeds the Five Thousand. [John 6:1_15].

Picture the scene on the shore of the Sea of Galilee where a great crowd gathered in awe of Jesus' miracle of restoring health to the sick. It's lunch time, the Jewish people are hungry, and there's no restaurant for miles. What's Jesus to do? "Eight month's wages would not be enough money to buy enough food for every person to have just one bite," exclaims Philip! "Have the people sit down," said Jesus. The miracle of blessing and expanding the five loaves of bread and the two fish is hard to believe, but it happened. And there were enough left_overs to feed many more people. Satisfied with full stomachs, the people were ready to make him king by force, if necessary, but they did not know what Jesus was all about. Even though Jesus met their immediate need then, he knew their inner thoughts and withdrew himself from their midst. Why would he do that? Had Jesus missed a great opportunity to reveal his Father? What would be the mindset of those whom Jesus fed? Were most of them glad he had met their need? Were there some disappointed that he left on short notice and wasn't around to feed them breakfast the next morning? Did they like him only when their stomachs were full?

The Disciples on the Lake near Capernaum. [John 6:16_24].

Strong winds, rough waters, and a dark night can add up to a stressful adventure. And then to observe Jesus walking on the water towards their boat, who wouldn't be terrified? Everyone knows that Jesus is breaking the law, the law of gravity, anyway! People are able to swim and float in the water, but Jesus is walking on the water, and he's hardly getting wet from the wind and the waves that are causing havoc for the disciples. With calm assurance Jesus enters the boat, and immediately they reach the other shore together in the boat. Jesus has just broken another law, the law of physics. A boat in the middle of a lake with several men onboard, and somehow they arrive on the other shore in a brief minute measurement of time. How could it happen? Some sort of energy propelled the boat and its occupants at a high rate of speed over the water. No doubt this is an amazing feat that boggles the mind, except for the fact that Jesus was present at the time. Surely the disciples were impressed with the power that Jesus exhibited at this juncture in their relationship with him.

The Man Born Blind. [John 9:1_41].

Being blind or deaf would certainly cause one to become frustrated with life in general, and perhaps become frustrated with God also. It would be so easy to blame him for not having all of the senses that most everyone else possesses. The man born blind is no exception. From the scripture account of this man and the things that happened to him, to his parents, to the religious community surrounding him, much can be written. For the purpose of this article, the point to be emphasized is the blind man's statement as to what he said to Jesus when he found out that it was Jesus who had given him his sight. The man said, "Lord, I believe." All Jesus wanted from the blind man was for the man to know him, to recognize that Jesus was God.

The Shepherd and His Flock. [John 10:1_42].

Sheep, a watchman, a shepherd, the sheep pen, strangers, thieves, hired hands, wolves _ a cast of characters that somehow tell a story. This creative narrative has much to say and reveal about God (the good shepherd), about people (the sheep), about evil (the thieves, the robbers and the wolf), and about the indifferent (the hired hand). Is there anyone left out? It appears that all are accounted for in this expose.

The people who are being exposed to Jesus reciting this story are the Jews. It is difficult for them to accept what he is relaying to them, even though he had just healed a man born blind. For many, their attitude toward Jesus is one of accusation, that Jesus is actually demon_possessed and raving mad. "Why listen to him?" they ask.

Jesus' sheep are just the opposite _ they are willing listen to Jesus' voice, the voice of the shepherd who goes ahead of them. They follow Jesus because they recognize his voice, and the sheep will never follow a stranger for just the opposite reason _ they don't recognize his voice. Listening is the key to knowing who you are following. Sheep are grateful for their shepherd who takes care of them. They only have to trust him that he is doing the right thing.

Lazarus, Mary & Martha. [John 11:1_57].

Four days in the tomb certainly qualifies as ample time to be declared dead, and there was no doubt in Jesus' mind that friend Lazarus was indeed dead. Jesus himself declared "Lazarus is dead." The two sisters of Lazarus were devastated, especially since they knew Jesus could have prevented his death in the first place. Why hadn't Jesus responded to their request of Jesus' presence? Sadness enveloped both Mary and Martha, and sadness was also present with Jesus as he wept openly. With a loud voice Jesus brought life back to a once_dead body, and Lazarus once again breathed air into his lungs as he had previously experienced. With the words, "Lazarus, come out!" Jesus raised Lazarus to life. For Mary and Martha, having their brother back in the household would be joy unspeakable, not to mention how Lazarus himself must have felt. What better gift could Jesus give them than this!

Jesus' Mother, Mary. [John 19:25_27].

Jesus said to his mother Mary, "Dear woman, here is your son," and to the disciple he said, "Here is your mother." With those words Jesus placed the future care of his mother in the hands of the disciple John, knowing full well he would not be around to provide for her and knowing full well John would be responsible for her. Mary could only agree and be thankful for her son's act of kindness toward her.

The Demon possessed Man. [Mark 5:1_20].

"What is your name?" Jesus asked. "My name is Legion," replied the man, "for we are many." The region of the Gerasenes became the area where demons were transferred from a human being to that of a large herd of pigs, and when that happened, the pigs rushed down into the lake and drowned. This event caused great concern, not for the man from whom the demons were cast out, but for the huge loss of the local swine enterprise. The people begged Jesus to leave their region at once, lest he cause another kind of catastrophe. The man who was cured of being demon_ possessed may possibly have been blamed for causing the loss of the pigs because if it wasn't for him in the first place, this wouldn't have taken place. The man, though, could only be ecstatic as he sat there, dressed and in his right mind. Those who saw what had happened were afraid. Of what do you suppose they were afraid? Were they afraid of Jesus; were they afraid of the man who was cured?

A Dead Girl and a Sick Woman. [Mark 5:21_43].

The synagogue ruler named Jairus implored Jesus to heal his young daughter who was dying, but while on the way to visit Jairus' home, a woman with a bleeding problem proceeded to demonstrate her faith in God by touching the clothes that Jesus wore. It was the woman's faith that healed her, not the act of touching Jesus' clothes. As Jesus continued on his journey to Jairus' home, it was announced that the daughter was dead, but Jesus told them, "Don't be afraid; just believe." (In other words, "trust me!") Laughter was heard when Jesus told those present "The child is not dead but asleep." At Jesus' command the twelve year old girl stood up and walked around in the presence of her mother, father, and the disciples.

The Faith of a Syrophoenician Woman. [Mark 7:24_30].

Nationality differences do not limit or discourage Jesus from healing those who are in need. Such was the case of a Greek woman who was born in Syrian Phoenicia. With a young daughter occupied with a demon, the woman begged Jesus to drive the evil spirit out of her. Jesus granted her request, and when the woman returned home, the demon was gone.

The Deaf and Mute Man. [Mark 7:31_37].

Near Decapolis (the Ten Cities) a deaf and mute man was cured of his infirmities. With the use of sign language, Jesus foretold the man what was about to happen to him, that he was about to receive that which he lacked, namely his hearing and being able to speak. The people were overwhelmed with amazement at this achievement that Jesus performed.

Jesus Feeds 4,000, [Mark 8:1_21].

To demonstrate that Jesus was not prejudiced, at another gathering Jesus had fed 5,000 Jewish people, but in this episode Jesus fed 4,000 non_Jewish people. Seven loaves of bread and a few small fish were more than enough to satisfy the number involved. Remarkably there were seven baskets of leftovers after everyone had their fill. Surely the attitude of those present was one of thankfulness.

The Boy with an Evil Spirit. [Mark 9:14_32].

Unable to speak and controlled by a spirit that would cause the young boy to go into convulsions, the boy's father asked the disciples to drive out the evil spirit, but they were unable to do so, mainly because of unbelief. In reply to this situation Jesus said to those present that **"everything is possible for him who believes."**

Summary:

Jesus gave the Woman at the Well and the people of Sychar eternal life in the form of living water.

The Invalid at the Pool received complete healing and the 5,000 Jewish people on the mountainside received much needed food to satisfy their hunger.

The disciples on the lake beheld Jesus as he did things no other man could do: walk on water and energize a boat with awesome power.

Jesus restored sight to the Man Born Blind, a feat never before recorded.

For those who are his Sheep, Jesus the Good Shepherd provides not only protection from harm but provides the necessary nourishment for life.

In sight of many witnesses, Jesus raised his friend Lazarus, the brother of Mary and Martha, from the tomb.

Even while dying on the Cross, Jesus remembers his Mother by having her cared for in his absence.

Legions of demons are expelled from a man who was found later to be in his right mind.

Jairus' daughter was healed and alive again; the woman with the bleeding problem was cured.

The Syrophoenician woman returned home to find that the demon was gone from her daughter.

The deaf and mute man was able to communicate normally with other people.

The 4,000 non_Jewish people who were fed with the loaves of bread and a few fish were content for the time being.

The boy who suffered convulsions no longer experienced them. Jesus told the boy's father that **"everything is possible for him who believes."**

Conclusion:

Throughout his journey while on planet Earth, Jesus performed many seemingly miraculous acts, none the least of which are mentioned above. No doubt, an endless number of similar events actually took place and could have been recorded in addition to the ones contained in scripture, but, as the gospel writer John explains,

> **"These things are written that you may believe that Jesus is the Christ, the Son of God, and that by believing you may have life in his name."**
> **John 20:31.**

Was Jesus who he claimed to be? Was he the Son of God? Did he actually have all the power of the Universe at his disposal, at his fingertips? Did he reveal his Father in a satisfactory manner? Did he leave anything undone or incomplete?

The events that were recorded by the gospel writers John and Mark quoted in this article are evidence and proof of Jesus' character and also the character of his heavenly Father. Did this need to be revealed? Was it important? Absolutely, because the picture of God that people had was a twisted and maligned assessment, and the truth needed to be clearly defined and made known. Such was Jesus' mission _ to make God known.

Despite all of the "good things" that Jesus did for a wide spectrum of people from an equally wide spectrum of backgrounds, Jesus did not have much success in the end. Few were on his side and it seems even fewer chose to follow him. Have you ever wondered why? Jesus did many wonderful things, so why did so many reject him? Why didn't anyone besides the one criminal on the cross respond? No one asked for forgiveness, but he forgave everyone regardless. If you had been one of those individuals who had been on the receiving end of Jesus' blessing and had been cured of disease, or had been like the Man Born Blind who received his sight, or like Lazarus who was raised from the dead, or like the thousands who had been fed with a small amount of fish and bread, or like the Woman at the Well who had been given eternal life, what would you have done as you stood beneath the Cross and watched Jesus die? Would you have agreed with the religious community who demanded his death? Would you have been part of the insane mob yelling at the top of their voices "Crucify him! He has a devil?"

If you had been like any of the people mentioned above who experienced the various things Jesus did for them, would you still have had need to plead his blood for the forgiveness of your sins as it is done today? Would you still need Jesus as your mediator to intercede between yourself and the Father? If you receive the "living water," the truth about God that produces eternal life, wouldn't you look at the Cross as an inhumane method to end someone's life? Do you realize that Jesus gave eternal life to those who were willing to listen before he died on the Cross? If you had been like the Man Born Blind and had received your sight from Jesus as he did, would you exclaim as he did **"One thing I do know. I was blind but now I see."** Before he met Jesus, he had an incorrect picture of God, but afterward he could see perfectly. As it turned out, those who claimed they could see were actually blind.

Jesus came to tell us about God, to reveal his character, to make God known to those willing to listen. Tragically, not many listened, and as a result few believed what Jesus said. For the majority of supposedly followers of God, Jesus was not qualified to represent the God that those people supposedly worshiped. Rejection led to hatred, and it was then just a small step to crucifixion as a mind full of envy and hatred will soon unload its emotions by eliminating and eradicating the cause of the perceived problem. People without reason hated Jesus, and their only avenue that could deal with the situation was for Jesus to die. Insane, corrupt people influenced by Satan the devil wanted Jesus dead, and they succeeded in attaining their goal.

It seems that the people who believe Jesus, who trust him, who put their faith in him that he knows everyone better than we claim to know ourselves, would certainly not be involved in his death. If you believe the fact that when your teacher says $2 + 2 = 4$ is correct, you don't have to kill your teacher then, do you? Shouldn't it be the same with Jesus? If you believe what he says is truth, why then would you participate in his death? It's the people who believe that $2 + 2 = 3$ and the people who believe $2 + 2 = 5$, they are the ones who cannot stand the truth and refuse to believe otherwise, that $2 + 2 = 4$. The insanity of sin is clearly revealed in the death of Jesus.

Would you be willing to set aside all previous beliefs and listen to Jesus testify about his Father, and then decide for yourself whether he told the truth and whether you believe him or not? Would you trust Jesus to read the true intentions of your heart, and not rely on your own personal claims about self?

Believe what Jesus says promotes life!
Refuse to believe what Jesus says promotes death!

Can you imagine people having a picture of God that requires him to die?

"Everything is possible for him who believes!"

It's Time to Quit!

It's Time to
Quit using "I am a sinner" as a crutch, as an excuse.
Get on with life! Know God as he really is!
Realize that God forgave you all of your sins a long time ago,
even before you were born.

It's Time to
Get up off your knees. Quit being a beggar.
Ask God for wisdom and knowledge that you might know him better.
Become obedient _ a humble willingness to listen to God.

It's Time to
Quit being a submissive servant.
God wants you to be an understanding friend.

It's time to
Quit bragging: "I've been saved! I've been born again!"
"When I die, I know I'm going to heaven!"
If you can accurately read your own heart,
what purpose is there for God?
Are you usurping God's prerogative?
Trust God that he knows character.
Stop resting on your own laurels.

It's time to
Quit putting yourself in place of God.
What you claim to know about yourself doesn't matter.
It's what God knows about you that determines everything.

Zacchaeus, the Tax Collector,
in the Sycamore Tree.

"An Oasis in the Desert"

Jesus entered Jericho and was passing through. A man was there by the name of Zacchaeus; he was a chief tax collector and was wealthy. He wanted to see who Jesus was, but being a short man he could not, because of the crowd. So he ran ahead and climbed a sycamore_fig tree to see him, since Jesus was coming that way.

When Jesus reached the spot, he looked up and said to him, "Zacchaeus, come down immediately. I must stay at your house today." So he came down at once and welcomed him gladly.

All the people saw this and began to mutter. "He has gone to be the guest of a 'sinner'."

But Zacchaeus stood and said to the Lord. "Look, Lord! Here and now I give half of my possessions to the poor, and if I have cheated anybody out of anything, I will pay back four times the amount."

Jesus said to him, "Today salvation has come to this house, because this man, too, is a son of Abraham. For the Son of Man came to seek and to save what was lost."

Luke 19:1_10

I've often wondered why Jesus chose Matthew instead of Zacchaeus, since they both had the same profession. Perhaps Jesus knew that Matthew would be the better gospel writer, that he would present certain information in a particular manner more in line with what needed to be said at the time. It is a bit odd to me that Matthew did not record the sycamore tree episode in his gospel, as there is a definite connection between the two men _ both were tax collectors.

Even by today's modern thoughts about people who are tax collectors, the average citizen still prefers to hold people with that occupation at arm's length. Unless a person knows the tax collector personally, usually the yearly or perhaps twice per year encounter with the tax collector is not an event to look forward to, nor one that it is deemed necessary to become acquainted with the person in charge. How many people do you know who cheerfully pay their tax allotment every year?

At the time of this event that happened two thousand years ago, disregard for tax collectors was probably on most people's mind. Somehow mistrust of funds paid to them became the means to label them as a "sinner." (v. 7). No doubt, a reputation built on suspicion by others was a hard one to live with, and Zacchaeus was no exception. It's no wonder they thought Jesus was crossing over the line when he entered the house of Zacchaeus. It appeared to them as though Jesus was about to scrape the bottom of the barrel!

Before Jesus arrived in Jericho, which was in proximity to Jerusalem, the news of his coming electrified the man Zacchaeus. This was all important to him, and nothing would deter him from seeing this Man. Perhaps Zacchaeus even closed the tax office that day, just so he could get a glimpse of Jesus. But being a man of short stature and with the immense crowd who likewise wanted to see Jesus, climbing the tree was his only chance. Of course, Jesus knew Zacchaeus would be there in the tree, but it was total surprise to Zacchaeus that Jesus called to him. Most people want nothing to do with tax collectors.

From Jesus' wording to Zacchaeus, it didn't leave much room, or any room for that matter, to disagree with Jesus. It appears that Jesus sort of invited himself, but there was happiness on the part of Zacchaeus. He appears to have been delighted! Not only was he called down from the tree by Someone whom he had never met and yet knew his name, but this same person was prepared to enter his house _ a feat that most citizens would never do because of tax collectors' reputations. This event showed to the average person that there was nothing to fear concerning tax collectors. They were honorable and honest people. This fact was proven immediately when Zacchaeus made his public statement: "Here and now I give half of my possessions to the poor, and if I have cheated anybody out of anything, I will pay back four times the amount." And to say this in front of Jesus and in front of the many people from whom he collected money, this was like finding **"an oasis in the desert."** It was quite refreshing to say the least!

Can you imagine the following words of Jesus being spoken to you? "Today salvation has come to this house, because this man, too, is a son of Abraham. For the Son of Man came to seek and to save what was lost."

How did salvation come to Zacchaeus' house? Did it come because Zacchaeus was a son of Abraham also? What is Jesus making known with this brief encounter, and why doesn't the conversation continue within the walls of Zacchaeus' house? Has everything been said that needed to be heard and recorded? It seems as though we are 'left in the dark' about some possible issues!

If salvation came to Zacchaeus' house that day, does that mean everyone inside was "saved?" Was that Jesus' intention? Jesus, of course, is salvation, and he came to the home of Zacchaeus much like he came to other people's homes. For instance, the home of Mary, Martha and Lazarus was frequented by Jesus often, as was the Upper Room also. Salvation did come to those houses as well, whenever Jesus was present.

With Zacchaeus' statement of honesty, does that fact mean he was "born again," that he was "saved?" What if, in the end, he paid back only three hundred per_cent and not the full four times the amount to those whom he was accused of cheating? Would he lose favor with God?

It seems somehow appropriate that this event happened just prior to the Triumphal Entry of Jesus riding a donkey into Jerusalem. It appears this occurred in the nick of time as there was now less than a week left of Jesus' ministry on earth. Why do you suppose this particular encounter with a tax collector was timed the way it was? And also, why would Jesus take the opportunity after speaking to Zacchaeus to tell the crowd gathered there about the Parable of the Ten Minas? How does that parable fit in with Zacchaeus in the sycamore tree?

Personal Reflection:

How difficult would it be to find another Zacchaeus in our world today? And he wouldn't even have to be a tax collector! In regard to Zacchaeus' pledge to return all monies that were taken dishonestly, I ask myself time and again: "Roger, would you be that bold? Do you have that much courage? Would you commit yourself to the extent that Zacchaeus did? If not, do you have a problem then? What is holding you back?"

I Tell You the Truth

[Introduction]

It seems to me that when Jesus says "I tell you the truth…" something of vital importance is about to be made known. For the listener it is an opportunity to pay special attention to what Jesus is about to say, not that whenever Jesus speaks a person should not pay attention, but this emphasis means something of significance is about to be revealed. In the New Testament, Matthew has 29, Mark has 12, Luke has 9 and John has 26 instances of Jesus saying "I tell you the truth…" That adds up to a total of 76 times.

This article records all of those instances. The verses where the words "I tell you the truth…" are found in the Bible have not been fully recorded here, but the chapter and verse are listed.

In New International Versions of the Bible, the four gospels contain a total of 3,778 verses. Of that total, 1,969 verses contain Jesus' conversations with others, and for me, listening to his words is a priority!

Peter said to Jesus:
"Lord, to whom shall we go? You have the words of eternal life." John 6:68.

<u>Want to know what is truth</u>? <u>Listen to Jesus</u>!

Jesus testified while standing before Pilate:
"Everyone on the side of truth listens to me." John 18:37.

I Tell You The Truth...

[Matthew]

5:18   until heaven and earth disappear, not the smallest letter, not the least stroke of a pen, will by any means disappear from the Law until everything is accomplished.

5:26   you will not get out until you have paid the last penny.

6:2   they have received their reward in full.

6:5   they have received their reward in full.

6:16   they have received their reward in full.

8:10   I have not found anyone in Israel with such great faith.

10:15   it will be more tolerable for Sodom and Gomorrah on the day of judgment than for that town.

10:23   you will not finish going through the cities of Israel before the Son of Man comes.

10:42   he will certainly not lose his reward.

11:11   among those born of women there has not risen anyone greater than John the Baptist; yet he who is least in the kingdom of heaven is greater than he.

13:17   many prophets and righteous men longed to see what you see but did not see it, and to hear what you hear but did not hear it.

16:28   some who are standing here will not taste death before they see the Son of Man coming in his kingdom.

17:20   if you have faith as small as a mustard seed, you can say to this mountain, "Move from here to there" and it will move. Nothing will be impossible for you.

18:3   unless you change and become like little children, you will never enter the kingdom of heaven.

18:18   whatever you bind on earth will be bound in heaven, and whatever you loose on earth will be loosed in heaven.

19:23   it is hard for a rich man to enter the kingdom of heaven.

19:28   at the renewal of all things, when the Son of Man sits on his glorious throne, you who have followed me will also sit on twelve thrones, judging the twelve tribes of Israel.

21:21   if you have faith and doubt not, not only can you do what was done to the fig tree, but also you can say to this mountain, "Go throw yourself into the sea," and it will be done.

21:31   the tax collectors and the prostitutes are entering the kingdom of God ahead of you.

23:36   all this will come upon this generation.

24:2   not one stone here will be left on another; every one will be thrown down.

24:32   this generation will certainly not pass away until all these things have happened.

24:47	he will put him in charge of all his possessions.
25:12	I don't know you.
25:40	whatever you did for the least of these brothers of mine, you did for me.
25:45	whatever you did not do for one of the least of these, you did not do for me.
26:13	wherever this gospel is preached throughout the world, what she has done will also be told, in memory of her.
26:21	one of you will betray me.
26:34	this very night, before the rooster crows, you will disown me three times.

I Tell You The Truth...

[Mark]

3:28 all the sins and blasphemies of men will be forgiven them. But whoever blasphemies against the Holy Spirit will never be forgiven; he is guilty of an eternal sin.

8:12 no sign will be given it.

9:1 some who are standing here will not taste of death before they see the kingdom of God come with power.

9:41 anyone who gives you a cup of cold water in my name because you belong to Christ will certainly not lose his reward.

10:15 anyone who will not receive the kingdom of God like a little child will never enter it.

10:29 no one who has left home or brothers or sisters or mother or father or children or fields for me and the gospel will fail to receive a hundred times as much in this present age (homes, brothers, sisters, mothers, children and fields – and with them persecution) and in the age to come, eternal life. But many who are first will be last, and the last first.

11:23 if anyone says to this mountain, "Go, throw yourself into the sea," and does not doubt in his heart but believes that what he says will happen, it will be done for him.

13:30 this generation will certainly not pass away until all these things have happened.

14:9 wherever the gospel is preached throughout the world, what she has done will also be told, in memory of her.

14:18 one of you will betray me – one who is eating with me.

14:25 I will not drink again of the fruit of the vine until that day when I drink it anew in the kingdom of God.

14:30 today, yes, tonight, before the rooster crows twice, you yourself will deny me three times.

I Tell You The Truth...

[Luke]

4:24   no prophet is accepted in his hometown.

9:27   some who are standing here will not taste death before they see the kingdom of God.

12:37   he will dress himself to serve, will have them recline at the table and will come and wait on them.

12:44   he will put them in charge of all his possessions.

18:17   anyone who will not receive the kingdom of God like a little child will never enter it.

18:29   no one who has left home or wife or brothers or parents or children for the sake of the kingdom of God will fail to receive many times as much in this age, and in the age to come, eternal life.

21:3   this poor widow has put in more than all the others.

21:32   this generation will certainly not pass away until all these things have happened.

23:43   today, you will be with me in paradise.

I Tell You The Truth...

[John]

1:51	you shall see heaven open, and the angels of God ascending and descending on the Son of Man.
3:3	no one can see the kingdom of God unless he is born again.
3:5	no one can enter the kingdom of God unless he is born of water and the Spirit.
3:11	we speak of what we know, and we testify of what we have seen, but still you people do not accept our testimony.
5:24	whoever hears my word and believes him who sent me has eternal life and will not be condemned; he has crossed over from death to life.
5:25	a time is coming and has now come when the dead will hear the voice of the Son of God and those who hear will live.
6:26	you are looking for me, not because you saw the miraculous signs, but because you ate the loaves and had your fill.
6:32	it is not Moses who has given you the bread from heaven, but it is my Father who gives you the true bread from heaven.
6:47	he who believes has everlasting life.
6:53	unless you eat the flesh of the Son of Man and drink his blood, you have no life in you.
8:34	everyone who sins is a slave to sin.
8:51	if anyone keeps my word, he will never see death.
8:58	before Abraham was born, I Am!
10:1	the man who does not enter the sheep pen by the gate, but climbs up by some other way, is a thief and a robber.
10:7	I am the gate for the sheep.
12:24	unless a kernel of wheat falls to the ground and dies, it remains only a single seed. But if it dies, it produces many seeds.
13:16	no servant is greater than his master, nor is a messenger greater than the one who sent him.
13:20	whoever accepts anyone I send accepts me; and whoever accepts me accepts the one who sent me.
13:21	one of you is going to betray me.
13:28	before the rooster crows, you will deny me three times.
14:12	anyone who has faith in me will do what I have been doing.
16:7	it is for your good that I am going away.

16:20 you will weep and mourn while the world rejoices. You will grieve, but your grief will turn to joy.

16:23 my Father will give you whatever you ask in my name.

21:18 when you were younger you dressed yourself and went where you wanted, but when you are old you will stretch out your hands, and someone else will dress you and lead you where you do not want to go.

The Faith Chapter

[Hebrews 11]

Appropriately called The Faith Chapter, Hebrews 11 is an interesting part of the Book of Hebrews. "By faith" important men and women of the Old Testament achieved notoriety and were looked upon and often revered as icons and representatives of God. Their place in the history of Biblical record is well documented and recognized; they were some of the giants of religious thought.

This article, entitled The Faith Chapter, is a lesson study complete with questions and answers. Perhaps a better word instead of answers would be observations as the material provided as answers is just the conclusion of those people participating in the study. These observations are written to clarify and add meaning to the verses under consideration. Realize these observations and conclusions would be best used as additional information and that they are the consensus of the group of people who studied together. Hopefully, the reader of this book will gain insight by reading through this chapter and by adding his own interpretation as to the meaning of the verses under consideration.

Hebrews 11 + 12

Faith _ Trust _ Belief

Abel, Enoch, Noah, Abraham, Isaac, Jacob, Joseph, Moses, Rahab, Gideon, Barak, Samson, Jephthah, David, Samuel, the prophets.

These were all commended for their faith, yet none of them received what had been promised. God had planned something better for us so that only together with us would they be made perfect.

Heb. 11:39, 40

<u>Heb. 12:1</u>. Therefore, since we are surrounded by such a great cloud of witnesses, let us throw off everything that hinders and the sin that so easily entangles, and let us run with perseverance the race marked out for us.

1. ...a great cloud of witnesses...
   Who are these witnesses? Are they not those people mentioned in the preceding chapter, beginning with Abel and ending with the prophets?

2. ...everything that hinders and the sin that so easily entangles...
   What is everything that hinders? Could that be our unbelief?
   What is the sin that entangles? Could that be the lies about God?

3. ...run with perseverance the race...
   What is the race? Could it be to maintain trust, faith, and belief?

<u>Heb. 12:2, 3</u>. Let us fix our eyes of Jesus, the author and perfecter of our faith, who for the joy set before him endured the cross, scorning its shame, and sat down at the right hand of the throne of God. Consider him who endured such opposition from sinful men, so that you will not grow weary and lose heart.

1. ...fix our eyes on Jesus...
   What do we see when we see Jesus? We see God!

2. **... who for the joy set before him...**

   What is the joy? We see God as he really is!

3. **...endured the cross...**

   Jesus struggled against the lie about God until it killed him. The Cross showed what lies were and what lies could do.

4. **...endured such opposition from sinful men...**

   Jesus demonstrated for all to see what the Father was like, even though it caused rejection every step of the way.

Heb. 12:3 6. In your struggle against sin, you have not yet resisted to the point of shedding your blood. And you have forgotten that word of encouragement that addresses you as sons: "My son, do not make light of the Lord's discipline, and do not lose heart when he rebukes you, because the Lord disciplines those he loves, and he punishes everyone he accepts as a son."

1. **...your struggle against sin...**

   What is the sin? Could it be the incorrect picture of God, perpetrated by Satan, the devil?

2. **...that word of encouragement...**

   The following quote is by Solomon found in Proverbs 3:11, 12.

Heb. 12:7 11. Endure hardship as discipline; God is treating you as sons. For what son is not disciplined by his father? If you are not disciplined (and everyone undergoes discipline), then you are illegitimate children and not true sons. Moreover, we have all had human fathers who disciplined as and we respected them for it. How much more should we submit to the Father of our spirits and live! Our fathers disciplined us for a little while as they thought best; but God disciplines us for our good, that we may share in his holiness. No discipline seems pleasant at the time, but painful. Later on, however, it produces a harvest of righteousness and peace for those who have been trained by it.

1. **...submit to the Father...**

   Be willing to listen to Jesus tell you about the Father.

2. **...a harvest of righteousness...**

   Do right because it is right, and leave the consequences with God!

3. **...and peace...**

   Peace and security between God and us.

Heb. 12:12 14. Therefore, strengthen your feeble arms and weak knees. Make level paths for your feet, so that the lame may not be disabled, but rather healed. Make every effort to live in peace with all men and to be holy; without holiness no one will see the Lord.

1. **...Make level paths for your feet...**
   Make every effort to live in peace with all men.

2. **...and to be holy...**
   To live in peace with God.

Heb. 12:15 17. See to it that no one misses the grace of God and that no bitter root grows up to cause trouble and defile many. See that no one is sexually immoral, or is godless like Esau, who for a single meal sold his inheritance rights as the oldest son. Afterward, as you know, when he wanted to inherit this blessing, he was rejected. He could bring about no change of mind, though he sought the blessing with tears.

1. **...the grace of God...**
   God's graciousness; God's character.

2. **...no bitter root...**
   no misunderstanding between men.

3. **...godless like Esau...**
   Esau (godless) had no interest in God; loved money, power, etc.
   Jacob (Godly) had interest in God; was family leader; had right attitude.

4. **...no change of mind...**
   A hardened heart; information rejected. God cannot do anything else.
   Esau, Lucifer, evil angels in the same category.

Heb. 12:18 21. You have not come to a mountain that can be touched and that is burning with fire; to darkness, gloom and storm; to a trumpet blast or to such a voice speaking words that those who heard it begged that no further word be spoken to them, because they could not bear what was commanded: "If even an animal touches the mountain, it must be stoned." The sight was so terrifying that Moses said: "I am trembling with fear."

Old Testament attitude: Fear brought on the sacrificial ceremonial system. It
   wasn't what God wanted, but it reminded the people who God was.
Also included is the Old Covenant: "All that the Lord has said, we will do."
The Old Covenant was founded upon the promises of people.

Heb. 12:22 24. But you have come to Mount Zion, to the heavenly Jerusalem, the city of the living God. You have come to thousands upon thousands of angels in joyful assembly, to the church of the firstborn, whose names are written in heaven. You have come to God, the judge of all men, to the spirits of righteous men made perfect, to Jesus the mediator of a new covenant, and to the sprinkled blood that speaks a better word than the blood of Abel.

> New Testament attitude: In their hearts and minds.
> Also included is the New Covenant: "God will put it in our minds, our hearts."
> The New Covenant was founded upon the promises of God.

1. **...thousands upon thousands of angels...**
   Thousands of angels convinced about Jesus and God.

2. **...church of the firstborn...**
   Those who have a spiritual relationship.

3. **...made perfect...**
   The correct disposition (attitude) toward God.

4. **...sprinkled blood...**
   The true picture of God.

Heb. 12:25 27. See to it that you do not refuse him who speaks. If they did not escape when the refused him who warned them on earth, how much less will we, if we turn away from him who warns us from heaven? At that time his voice shook the earth, but now he has promised, "Once more I will shake not only the earth but also the heavens." The words "once more" indicate the removing of what can be shaken _ that is, created things _ so that what cannot be shaken may remain.

1. **...I will shake not only the earth but also the heavens...**
   Shake the earth _ the incorrect picture of God.
   Shake the heavens _ the correct picture of God.

2. **...created things...**
   A reference to everything except God.

Heb. 12:28, 29. Therefore, since we are receiving a kingdom that cannot be shaken, let us be thankful, and so worship God acceptably with reverence and awe, for our "God is a consuming fire."

1. **...with reverence and awe...**
   Why? Because we got the correct picture of God.

2. **..."God is a consuming fire."**
   Fire = Light, Energy, Power.
   > Light _ correct information about God.
   > Energy _ to move, to grow, to change.
   > Power _ to change one's mind; to transform thinking.

First Covenant.
1. **An example of what doesn't work!**
2. **Didn't tell people what God was like.**
3. **Priests didn't know God either.**

New Covenant (New Order).
1. **An example of what really works!**
2. **A time of setting straight, getting it right.**

Good Things.
1. **A beautiful picture of God.**

Eternal Redemption.
1. **Rescue from untruths, from lies about God.**
   a. **God doesn't kill; people draw away from him.**

   Death is a component of sin. The wages of sin is death.
   > **Sin _ don't understand what is true about God.**

The Blood

What does it mean when Jesus' blood is mentioned in scripture?
Does it mean his literal blood?
Could "his blood" have a different meaning?

Criminals often have to pay for their crimes with their own blood, don't they? In other words, the penalty for the crime that they commit means the end of their life. Do the crime; suffer the penalty! Some of today's severe criminal cases end in death by modern methods: electrocution, gas chamber, chemical injection. Previous methods meant: a rope around the neck, a bullet through the brain or heart; a slow and painful death on a cross. The intended end result was always the same though: death.

I do not believe when scripture talks about Jesus' blood that in every instance it means his literal blood. I do believe, however, that when people are angry and mad at someone else, enough so that they want to silence and/or kill the other person, the literal blood of that person is what they want, because without literal blood in a physical body, there can be no life. Read Lev. 17:11, 14. In other words, Blood = Life. What happened to Jesus when his body was drained of blood? He died; his life ended. No Blood = No Life!

What causes anger and madness in people? Why are some people upset with other people? I submit to you that it's because the other people do not believe what they want them to believe, and/or it's because the other people are not doing what they want them to do. This is an attitude problem that has evolved since Creation, and the battle has raged on since that time. It comes down to one word in my way of thinking _ control. And control of the mind is the issue. If you control the mind, you control the actions.

To start at the beginning, I would start with Jesus' Mission: to reveal his Father. For instance, the gospel writer John is explicit in his purpose for writing his book. His purpose is found in John 1:18 at the start of his book and in John 17:25, 26, the last two sentences of Jesus' prayer before being betrayed by Judas. Quotes: "No one has ever seen God, but God the One and Only, who is at the Father's side, has made him known." (1:18). "Righteous Father, though the world does not know you, I know you, and they know that you have sent me. I have made you known to them, and will continue to make you known in order that the love you have for me may be in them and that I myself may be in them." (17:25, 26). Can it be stated then that between these two verses, John the gospel writer "has made God known?" I believe he has, like no other book in the Bible.

Jesus' Mission then is to reveal his Father, to "make his Father known." Dare we ask why this might be important and necessary? Was it due to the fact that the most religious people of the day, (in fact, they were God's chosen people), had the wrong picture of God and what God was all about? Jesus came to present, to testify, and to demonstrate what God was like, and that he was

God's true representative (Heb. 1:3). But we all know what happened. He was totally rejected by those who claimed to be his own.

Jesus' Mission, his work, was not to "die on the Cross," and to "shed his blood." I believe this because of Jesus' prayer to his Father in John 17. In John 17:4, Jesus prays: "I have brought you glory on earth by completing the work you gave me to do." If Jesus has completed the work that the Father gave him to do before the Crucifixion, doesn't that eliminate the Cross as being part of that work? I believe it does. God's work for Jesus was to "make God known." This is further explained in John 18:37 as Jesus stands before Pilate. "You are a king, then!" said Pilate. Jesus answered, "You are right in saying I am a king. In fact, for this reason I was born, and for this I came into the world, to testify to the truth. Everyone on the side of truth listens to me." WOW! What a testimony! Why did Jesus testify to the truth? Were there a lot of lies about his Father to be found? Did Jesus "come to die?" Could it be that he came to tell us about God, to testify to the truth? Could it be that if everyone had been on Jesus' side they would have listened to him and would not have demanded his death? It's no wonder that Jesus told the disciples beforehand about this class of people: "They hated me without reason." John 15:25. Read more about this hatred in John 15:18_27. The Cross was the result of the impact Jesus had on people's lives and what they believed. Imagine: insane religious people who thought they knew God, and they hated him without reason!

If Jesus' sole purpose for coming was "to die for our sins," then what he said about his Father had no relevance, and people would have had no reason to kill him. Hypothetically, could Jesus have just lived a quiet and recluse life of 80 years or so, died of some disease or natural cause, or by some accident? Would his death then have been sufficient? Why or why not? If all that was needed and necessary was for him "to die for our sins," it seems as though he went out of his way to make it happen.

Is there no forgiveness from God for anyone unless and until Jesus sheds his blood? Scripture says, "...without the shedding of blood, there is no forgiveness." (Heb. 9:22). Remember, the Hebrew people were still offering animal blood sacrifices according to the ceremonial law when Jesus was on earth. One would think that taking the life of an innocent lamb, or a dove, etc. would have an effect on people's minds, but they didn't understand and they refused to listen to God. It became a bloody ceremony of no value, and it later became a small, easy step from slaying animals to taking the life of Jesus. People wouldn't listen as Jesus revealed his Father to them; neither would they listen to God centuries before. "Moses, you talk to God; God, you talk to Moses; then Moses, you talk to us and tell us what God said!" Why were people afraid of God then? Why are people afraid of God today? We still have and can see and experience the same "watered_down" effect in much of today's religious community. "Why not let someone else be the 'go_between,' the mediator between God and individuals? I'm afraid of God! I don't want to be bothered with it!" I say: "Yuk! It's not what God wants."

Jesus' Blood represents Jesus' unwillingness to tell a lie about his Father. Jesus told the truth about God; it cost him his life! Hypothetically, could and would the same thing happen today? In my opinion: Yes, without a doubt!

The four gospels record several instances of Jesus saying: "I tell you the truth..." I believe each of these "truths" says something about God. Matthew has 29; Mark has 12; Luke has 9; and John has 26. Why would Jesus start a conversation with those words? Would it be because he was placing special emphasis on what he was about to say? Could it be in some cases because there was an opposing "untruth" that needed to be exposed? Look them up sometime; it's good reading!

John 6:53 56. Jesus said to them: "I tell you the truth, unless you eat the flesh of the Son of Man and drink his blood, you have no life in you. Whoever eats my flesh and drinks my blood has eternal life, and I will raise him up at the last day. For my flesh is real food and my blood is real drink."
If Jesus' blood is literal, how do we do this today? Where do we go to get it?

Revelation 7:14. And he said. "These are they who have come out of the great tribulation; they have washed their robes and made them white in the blood of the Lamb."
A lot of people come out of the tribulation. Will there be enough blood to go around? Will it somehow have to be diluted? I hope there are enough washing machines in Heaven to go around! What does this statement really mean?

Hebrews 9:22. "...without the shedding of blood there is no forgiveness."
Does that mean what it says? Has no one on this planet been forgiven since Day One, since Creation? No forgiveness until Jesus died on the Cross? What about the paralytic man of Luke 5:20? "When Jesus saw their faith, he said, 'Friend, your sins are forgiven'." Also, Luke 7:48, concerning the woman with the alabaster box who anointed Jesus' feet, states: "Then Jesus said to her, 'Your sins are forgiven'" Evidently, Jesus could forgive sins at his discretion, and he did not have to die first.

Matthew 26:27, 28. "While they were eating, Jesus took bread, gave thanks and broke it, saying, 'Take and eat; this is my body.' Then he took the cup, gave thanks and offered it to them, saying, 'Drink from it, all of you. This is my blood of the covenant, which is poured out for many for the forgiveness of sins."

1 Corinthians 11:23 26. "For I received from the Lord what I also passed on to you: The Lord Jesus on the night he was betrayed, took bread, and when he had given thanks, he broke it and said, 'This is my body, which is for you; do this in remembrance of me.' In the same way, after supper he took the cup, saying, 'This cup is the new covenant in my blood; do this, whenever you

drink it, in remembrance of me.' For whenever you eat this bread and drink this cup, you proclaim the Lord's death until he comes."

Is Communion the only time we receive forgiveness of sins? Who of us can accurately and know without a doubt what all of our sins are? Can we name them all and not leave any out? What happens if we inadvertently omit one or two? Wait till next time? What if we would happen to die in the mean time and hadn't asked God to be forgiven for those sins? Would we be lost?

Closing Statements.

1. I believe Jesus and his Father are forgiveness personified, that they have forgiven us even before we sin. Like the Prodigal Son, his father forgave him before he left home, before he lost his inheritance in riotous living, and before he found himself hungry and living with a bunch of pigs. The Prodigal Son put on his thinking cap and "came to his senses" (Luke 15:17). What conclusion did he come to? His father was right all along! God is just like that with us! He forgives us before we begin our journey of life. That's the kind of God he is!

If we believe what Jesus tells us about his Father, why do we need his blood? We have to kill him in order to get his blood, don't we? It seems like that is the only way possible. Did the Father enjoy seeing his only Son die? It's like if I wanted to convince you that 2 plus 2 equals 4, and you agree that, yes, that is correct. Then why would I have to die? You believe what I told you. What more needs to be done? I'm not forcing you or strong_arming you to accept what I'm telling you. It's your choice whether to believe it or not. It's just that it is right and that it makes sense, that 2 plus 2 equals 4, doesn't it?

If we don't believe what Jesus tells us about his Father, blood is the ultimate requirement to satisfy our insane envy and hatred. We just cannot stand it when someone else has found flaws in our belief system and has revealed that we have believed a lie. Such, though, was the position of religious people 2,000 years ago. Has much changed since then? The same lie that was present at Creation was present then, and it's still present today, in my opinion.

2. The Cross demonstrates the consequence of being believers in the wrong picture of God and what those believers will do to those who believe otherwise. The consequence of those believers says: get rid of those who present God in a different light.

The Cross reveals the insanity of sin, the refusal to accept the picture of God as revealed by Jesus. Sin will even kill the One who gives life to everything and everyone. If Jesus hadn't come to tell us about his Father, how would we have known what he was like? Jesus is the express image, the exact representation of the Father.

3. Jesus came to testify and reveal the truth about his Father. Jesus claimed that he is "the Way, the Truth, and the Life." (John 14:6). He also said: "Everyone on the side of truth listens to me." (John 18:37).

We need to make sure we are on his side, the side of truth. Listen to Jesus as he reveals truth about his Father. All he asks of us is that he be given the opportunity to present that information about God, and he leaves it up to us whether to accept or reject that information. Being the kind of person that he is, he will honor both decisions equally, because it is this freedom of choice that forms the basis of his government. He will not force himself upon anyone.

CHAPTER 40

Truth About God

The search for truth about God must begin with Jesus, for he said:

"All things have been committed to me by my Father.
No one knows the Son except the Father, and no one knows the Father except the Son,
and those to whom the Son chooses to reveal him."

Matthew 11:27.

What is the truth about God? Who does Jesus reveal?

1. We don't know God.

   a. God sent Jesus to make him known. John 1:18; 17:26.
   b. Jesus' teachings are truth that sets us free from Satan's lies.
   c. Jesus' death and resurrection sets us free from our fear of death.
   d. The knowledge that Jesus gives = eternal life. John 17:3.

2. God knows us.

   a. Jesus and Nathaniel. John 1:43_51.
   b. Jesus and the woman of Sychar. John 4:4_38.
   c. Jesus knows what is in man.

3. God loves us and wants us to live. 1 John 4:16.

4. God can be approached.

   a. Jesus said he would never drive anyone away. John 6:37.

5. Eternal Life = our knowledge of God. John 17:3.

   a. It is the way we live, not the length of life.

6. Judgment is about God, not us.

   a. It is our decision whether to accept or reject God.

7. Jesus' death was demanded by created beings, not by the Creator.

8. Sin involves a lie about God.

9. Guilt is pronounced when people prefer the lies instead of the truth about God.

10. Salvation is based on what God knows about us, not on what we demonstrate.

Key Elements to the Truth About God

Jesus Mission:

Jesus came to this world to reveal the character and desires of God; to demonstrate relationship, what it means and how it works; to change people from independence to interdependence; to deliver individuals from fear and to restore them to friendship.

A. Revealing God.
   1. "No one has ever seen God, but God the One and Only, who is at the father's side has made him known." John 1:18.
   2. "I have brought you glory on earth by completing the work you gave me to do...I have revealed you..." John 17:4_6.
   3. The One from heaven _ "the Son of Man." John 3:13.
   4. My Father – "Though you do not know him, I know him." John 8:58.

B. A Perfect Relationship.
   1. The Father loves Jesus and gives him total control. John 3:35.
   2. Jesus loves his Father and does whatever his Father asks of him. John 14:31.

C. Interdependence.
   1. Jesus did nothing by himself. John 5:19; 8:26.
   2. No one can represent God unless he depends on God. John 15:4.
   3. Our interdependence testifies to God's love and presence. John 17:20_23.

D. Fear vs. Friendship.
   a. Free from fear. Hebrews 2:14, 15; John 7:12, 13.
   b. Friendship of God. John 15:13_15.

II. Jesus' Message:

Everything Jesus did, both his words and his actions, communicates something to us about God. Jesus didn't just speak a message _ he was the message. When we read what he said, these are the words that his Father would say. When we see how Jesus treated people, the Father would have responded in the same manner.

A. Opening Statement. John 3:16, 17.
    1. God loves the world.
    2. God wants people to live.
    3. God sent Jesus to save, not to condemn.
        a. Jesus consistently spoke about how good God is, not how bad we are.

B. Demonstration of Love, Acceptance, and Forgiveness.
    1. "If you knew me, you would ask for 'living water' and I would give it to you." John 4:10; 7:36, 37.
    2. "You may go. Your son will live." John 4:46_53.
    3. "Do you want to get well?" John 5:5_8.
    4. "I am willing...Be clean!" Mark 1:40_42.

C. God wants to give life and freedom.
    1. Full life; unlimited freedom. John 10:9, 10.
    2. "If the Son sets you free, you will be free indeed." John 8:36.
    3. "It is for freedom that Christ has set us free." Galatians 5:1.

D. God sent Jesus, his Son, to save, not to condemn.
    1. "I do not condemn you." John 8:11.
    2. "Jesus told me everything I ever did," but he didn't condemn me! John 4:29.
    3. No condemnation in Christ. Set free. Romans 8:1, 2.

E. "The one whom God has sent speaks the words of God..." John 3:34.
    1. "Whoever hears my word and believes him who sent me has eternal life and will not be condemned; he has crossed over from death to life. John 5:24.
    2. "Anyone who has seen me has seen the Father." John 14:9.

III. Salvation and Eternal Life:

Salvation comes to individuals when they believe that Jesus spoke the truth about his Father; when they believe Jesus correctly represented his Father by the way he treated people, and when they choose to allow the God they have heard and seen participate in their lives. When that choice is made, a person receives eternal life, i.e. the way life will be lived for all eternity. Eternal life is the information we receive from God about the way people should live together, not the reward given at the judgment to those who have lived a "good life."

A. Jesus spoke and lived the message that his Father gave him.
1. Jesus did only what he saw his Father doing. John 5:19, 20.
2. The One whom God sent speaks the words of God. John 3:34.
3. What Jesus heard from his Father he told the world. John 8:26; 12:50.

B. Jesus as the "Word." John 1:1_3.
1. Jesus is described as the "Word" because he was a living communication from God. Everything about him revealed God. John 1:1_18.
2. If you see Jesus, you see God. John 14:9.
3. Jesus was the exact representation of God. Hebrews 1:1_3.

C. No condemnation.
1. Whoever believes in Jesus is not condemned. John 3:18.
2. Whoever believes in Jesus has eternal life. John 4:36.
3. Believe in Jesus; believe in God. See Jesus; see God. John 12:44, 45.

D. Eternal Life now.
1. Cross over from death to life at the moment of believing. John 5:24.
2. When we listen and follow, Jesus gives eternal life. John 10:27, 28.
3. Eternal Life is equal to knowing God. John 17:3.

IV. The Truth vs. the Lie (sin):

Jesus, who was continually in the presence of his Father, came to tell people, who have never been in the presence of his Father, about God. This was necessary because Satan (known also as Lucifer) had lied about God by distorting and confusing created beings as to God's purpose and intent. The resulting uncertainty about God is described as "darkness," which Jesus, as "light," came to dispel. This is the foundation of the struggle between good and evil, between Christ and Satan. The battlefield is the minds of individuals where a "war" is being waged for allegiance and trust. Who can be trusted?

A. Jesus _ the One and Only.
1. No one has ever seen God _ only Jesus has. John 1:18.
2. No one has been to heaven, except Jesus. John 3:13.
3. Jesus testifies to what he has seen and heard. John 3:31, 32; 8:14.

B. Jesus _ the Light; the Bearer of Truth.
1. Jesus is the light of the world to lead people out of darkness. John 8:12; 1:9; 3:19_21; 12:35, 36.
2. Jesus is the truth. John 14:6.
3. If we continue to listen to Jesus we will know truth. John 8:31, 32.
4. Jesus knows his Father; we do not. If Jesus said he didn't, he would lie. John 8:55.

C. Satan is the Father of lies.
1. A murderer, with no truth in him. John 8:44.
2. Those who make claims of God, apart from Jesus, perpetuate the lie. They are relying on hearsay evidence. John 8:38.
3. Those who use God for their own purposes love the darkness and hate the light because it exposes them for what they really are. John 3:19_21.

D. Sin, Satan's Lies, Enslaving the Mind.
1. The sinner is a slave to sin. John 8:34.
2. The truth sets one free from this slavery, if we listen. John 8:32, 36.
3. Those who belong to God will listen. Those who don't belong to God refuse to listen. John 8:47.
4. Jesus came to this world so that individuals could make a clear and informed decision whether to accept or reject God. John 9:39.

V. Judgment _ Guilt or Freedom:

The judgment is about the character of God and his purpose. He is the one who has been accused and, in a sense, is on trial before his Universe. The judgment vindicates the decisions and actions he has taken, restoring him to a position of trust. Jesus' primary task was to clarify the position of confused and frightened individuals concerning the judgment. The "good news" is: we are not on trial, but, rather, we have been given the opportunity to testify on God's behalf at his trial.

A. Judgment is about God.
   1. Eternal life is equal to knowing God. John 17:3.
   2. Jesus gives eternal life as a gift to all who accept the true knowledge about God. John 17:2; 5:22_24.
   3. Those who accept the true knowledge about God are described as already belonging to God before they heard the truth. John 17:2; 6:37_39; 10:16.
   4. Jesus came to this world so that decisions could be made about God. John 9:39.

B. Jesus _ Advocate for God and Man.
   1. Jesus testifies to the truth about his Father. John 17:4_6.
   2. Jesus judges all who believe his testimony, declaring them worthy of eternal life even when there is no apparent change in their behavior. John 5:22_24, 27.

C. The Father as Judge.
   1. The Father judges whether Jesus spoke what was true. John 8:50.
   2. The Resurrection of Jesus is God's judgment that he spoke the truth. Philippians 2:9_11.

D. The Obvious Judgment.
   1. When individuals reject the truth which Jesus spoke, it is obvious to everyone that their rejection of truth is their judge. John 12:31, 47, 48.

VI. The Cross _ Rejection and Death.

As the light of truth about God penetrated the darkness of Satan's lies, hatred grew in those individuals who saw their control, which they had gained from those lies, begin to disappear. In spite of all the evidence, they rejected Jesus as the Messiah and the life he offered. In their hatred, they endeavored to take the life of the Life Giver, God! The Cross is the cruel exclamation point to the truth revealed in Jesus' life. It stands as a grim reminder to the insanity of sin.

   A. Rejection _ The agony of Jesus.
1. Jesus was troubled by those he could not save. John 11:33; 12:27; 13:21.
2. "Why will you die?" Ezekiel 18:31, 32; 33:11.
3. Jesus came to save, but some were unwilling. Matt. 23:37; Hosea 11:7, 8.

   B. Insanity of Sin.
1. Hatred of Jesus because he exposed evil deeds. John 3:19, 20.
2. Hatred of Jesus because he would not choose them. John 15:18, 19.
3. Guilty of sin because they hated Jesus without reason. John 15:24, 25.

   C. The Work of God.
1. Jesus finished his Father's work before the Cross. John 17:4.
2. Satan sought to destroy Jesus because of the truth he revealed about God. The Cross reveals the true nature of Satan's desire, and he is driven out. John 14:30; 12:32.
3. In the battle of the mind, Jesus' death on the Cross becomes the ultimate act of protection. John 10:11_13.

Potpourri

Jesus didn't tell the thief on the cross that he needed to repent, that he needed to be 'born again,' that he needed to confess his sin, that he needed to beg for forgiveness. Jesus didn't berate him for his ignorance of not knowing God. Jesus told the thief that he was accepted just as he was. How could Jesus do that? What did Jesus know about the thief? Jesus knew the thief was willing to listen and learn.

Jesus didn't tell Nicodemus: "Unless you are washed in the blood, you'll not be saved!" Jesus told him he had the wrong picture of God.

Jesus did the demonstration of God's character. We report the demonstration.

<u>Jesus' Mission</u>: to set men right through the revelation of God's character.

<u>Forgetful God</u>? "I will remember their sins no more." Jer. 31:34. Does that mean God will suffer loss of memory? Alzheimer's? Will God truly "forget," or will he just not ever bring it up again?

<u>Satan's End Work</u>: to prepare the world to receive the counterfeit Christ. Is he doing a splendid job? Don't go looking in the saloons or on the golf course for that; look in the churches! Where are people talking about Christ and accepting him as their personal savior? And the signs and the wonders and miracles! Where are they making claims and extolling the work of the Holy Spirit more than in the churches, on television, in huge evangelistic endeavors, in global evangelism?

<u>The Foundation of God's Government</u>: <u>Freedom of Choice</u>. As God, what do you do with people who choose to go their own way?

A doctor cannot force his patients to be well. Neither can God, the Great Physician.
Jesus died for sinless angels as much as he died for sinful man.
Eating the apple in the Garden of Eden = Internalizing Satan's lies about God.

If Jesus would have donated his blood at the local Red Cross center instead of dying on the Cross, would that have been sufficient? If a needle was stuck in his arm and a pint of blood withdrawn from his body, would that satisfy the present_day religious community? What if Jesus had inadvertently scratched his arm and a drop or two of blood came out, would that have been enough? How much blood and how little blood does it take to satisfy blood_thirsty people?

If Jesus had been killed as a very young child by King Herod when he issued that decree to kill all male children under two years of age, would that death have been sufficient?

Jesus didn't come to reveal the truth about us. He came to reveal the truth about his Father, God.

The Cross was the final evidence to convince the angels about God's character.

<u>Language of a little child</u>: "Daddy, doesn't God love us as much as Jesus does?" And you the parent ask: "How could you raise that question? How could you ask that?" The child replies: "Well, Jesus is pleading with God to forgive me for the things I did wrong today, so I know who's on my side!"

<u>Protection in the Garden of Eden</u>. God said: "Don't go near that tree, because you will encounter someone who has deceived brilliant angels. What chance do you think you will have?"

<u>Trust</u>. Can trust be acquired by the demonstration of one act? Two acts? Ten acts? God's method: Trust is attained by demonstration over a long period of time and under a great variety of circumstances, particularly difficult ones.

<u>Prayer is not a substitute for Truth and Evidence</u>. The Holy Spirit cannot function if there is no interest in evidence.

<u>To be settled into the truth</u>. In your own life, when was the most stirring moment you have ever had when you thought about God? Was it at a gathering with loud raucous music and excitement? Or was it in a place where quiet consideration of evidence was presented? Where does the 'still, small voice' of the Holy Spirit of Truth work best?

Salvation was not the issue when the war in heaven began. The character of God was at stake.

<u>To "pray in Jesus' name."</u> If Jesus had not come to reveal his Father, we would not know the truth about God.

If we pray and claim God has blessed us, is that proof of God's approval of us? God is good even to his enemies, and the same rain falls on everyone.

"In one accord" (in total agreement) doesn't mean truth is being shared or witnessed. They all can be wrong! Is it possible to give a false witness with the Holy Spirit?

Does Jesus' forgiveness on the Cross mean everyone will be saved?

What is the greatest compliment you could offer to God?
Might it be: To be still... and to listen?

<u>"Safe to Save."</u> A person who places his trust in God, the Great Physician; that it is God alone who knows and can read the heart of an individual; and that it is not some person's belief that he has been saved.

Salvation is based upon what God knows, and not upon our own personal claims.

206

One of the main functions of formalized religion is to protect people against a direct experience with God.

<u>One of the marks of true spirituality</u>: <u>raise questions</u>! This was something Jesus desired from the disciples, but was seldom realized. If you are led by the Holy Spirit, he is the Spirit of Truth and Inquiry. Cut through the darkness of "dark speech," and get to the light of understanding.

The Cross demonstrates the consequences of being true believers in the wrong picture of God.

<u>Jesus' Work</u>: not to give rewards, but to give knowledge about God!

The only way to know God is to let him teach you!
There is great healing in honest conversation with God. There's no need to be afraid!
The diversity of religion is not the result of God's plan, but the result of sin at work in human hearts. Ironically, most of it has resulted from sinful people telling other sinful people how they are sinning.
Only when all eyes are focused of Jesus and the truth he reveals about his Father will the uniqueness of each individual no longer present a problem.

<u>The Cross</u>. The insanity of it all is clearly revealed for all to see, as those who are dependent on God for life scream for his death.

In heaven, will God have to apologize for not "giving in" to our requests? Will he have to give an account for all of his actions?
Do you believe there is one true church? If so, what are its marks of identification?
In scripture, God is often depicted as causing that which he does not prevent.

<u>Choose right because it is right, and leave the consequences with God</u>!

Faith is no leap in the dark. Faith is a decision to trust God based on unquestionable evidence.
To rebellious people who won't listen, God raises his voice (thunder, earthquake, fire). To others who are his friends, God can talk softly as he did to Elijah at the cave.
Pretentious Piety is nauseating to the Lord.

<u>Our Purpose</u>: to introduce people to the kind of person God is.

Religious people don't necessarily make the best neighbors. Some people are deeply religious, deep into creed, ritual, and ceremony, and they are down right cruel. In the name of religion they are cruel!
When God thundered on Sinai, the people were momentarily respectful, but they soon forgot it. When Jesus wept on the Mount of Olives, they weren't respectful at all. But when Jesus raised

his voice of Sinai, Moses stood there and thought to himself: "How marvelous that God would be willing to do that." People are not respectful of meekness. Moses respected meekness.

Why did the Lord thunder on Sinai and weep on the Mount of Olives? Which method seemed to work better? How many did he win on Sinai? How many did he win on the Mount of Olives? Neither seemed to work very well. Is the Lord searching for some method that will really work and hasn't hit upon it yet?

Throughout the Bible, God goes to almost extreme measures to demonstrate his power and whatever is appropriate to gain the attention of the people and hold it long enough to tell them the truth about himself, like: "I'd rather you be my understanding friends."

Has the religious community baptized the devil's accusations against God?

Is God arbitrary? God is non_negotiable and is immovably and dogmatically committed to one thing on which he will never budge _ freedom!

What if you went to Heaven right now and found where God was, and in your anger that he had not made things good for you, that some friends, relatives, and acquaintances are not in Heaven, and you were to go up to God and slap him and spit in his face, what will God do? Did anyone slap Jesus and spit in his face? Did anyone do that? They did it! Now, what did Jesus do? He said: "I forgive you!" That is the ultimate truth about God! That's the Good News!

God doesn't want to kill or destroy us. The Cross proves that we want to kill God!

The Cross is the final evidence of what God is like. God isn't killing people; people are killing God!

Obedience: a humble willingness to listen.

Obedience that springs from fear produces the character of a rebel.
People who kept the law killed Jesus.
Why does God wait? What is delaying Jesus' return? We're not settled into the truth!

Freedom. Present evidence about God and allow people the freedom of choice to accept or reject the information.

Sin _ don't understand what is true about God!

Can a person be accepted around the religious community as a wonderful representative of truth, but inside actually be God's adversary by misrepresenting the truth in very subtle and pious ways?

War in heaven divided the Universe.

God doesn't ask us to believe him because of who he is, but because he tells the truth, and he is willing to provide unquestionable evidence about that truth. If God the Father is forgiveness personified as Jesus is, why does he need someone (Jesus) to plead with him? Did anyone plead with Jesus on the Cross to forgive his tormentors?

The greatest sin anyone can commit is to misrepresent God.

Servants _ Sin is breaking the rules.

Understanding Friends _ Sin is misrepresenting God.

The Second Death. [1st Resurrection, 2nd Resurrection].

In the 1st Resurrection, all of the "saved" will be raised. They will forever be inhabitants of the New Heavens and later the New Earth.

In the 2nd Resurrection, all of the wicked, the "lost" will be raised. They will die the Second Death from which there is no resurrection; they will cease to exist.

The Second Death is not an endless life of torture and pain in the flames of hell that God has imposed upon wicked people. The Second Death is a complete and thorough discontinuation of life.

If all of the wicked are raised in the 2nd Resurrection to receive their reward of punishment (to burn for all eternity in the flames of hell), why would God resurrect the inhabitants of Sodom and Gomorrah to burn them again in the Second Death? Didn't he burn them long enough the first time?

Why hasn't Jesus returned as he promised? Why are we still here?

Could it be that we've bought into the devil's picture of God?

The Cross (Jesus' death) is the payment of a legal penalty to satisfy God's justice and to propitiate God's wrath. Who do you suppose smiles every time that statement is made? Answer: Satan, the devil, of course!

When you go to a medical physician, do you ask: "Doctor, what must I do to be forgiven?" No, you ask: "Doctor, what must I do to get well, to be healed?" Yet, in the realm of Christianity where patients have need for the Great Physician, most everyone wants only to be forgiven. God wants to heal people! Do you trust him enough to follow his instructions, some of which may be painful? Forgiveness doesn't change people from sinners into saints! We need to be renewed in our minds concerning what God is all about.

"If"

[the last four lines]

If you can fill the unforgiving minute
With sixty seconds' worth of distance run,
Yours is the Earth and everything that's in it,
And _ which is yours _ you'll be a Man, my son!

Kipling

Introduction to
"Vincent (Starry, Starry Night)"
Lyrics by Don McLean
Sung by Josh Groban

From the book of Genesis to the book of Revelation, it seems there are countless occasions where the word **"listen"** is written in scripture. In many instances God spoke the word **"listen"** in an imperative manner where it is a must, almost a command! Other times God spoke the word **"listen"** more gently as a means of getting his message across. Listening is the most basic method of communicating with someone else: one person talks, the other person listens. The tragedy that Jesus experienced during his ministry centered on the fact there were many who refused to listen, and also the fact there were others who were unable to understand what he was saying due to ingrained beliefs. As with most people the problem of communication was due to selective hearing.

**"They would not listen
They did not know how
Perhaps they'll listen now."**

The words to the song "Vincent" were written by Don McLean as a tribute and a portrait of the artist himself who painted "Starry Night" _ Vincent Van Gogh. The reader of this book is encouraged to read those words on the next page, and while doing so reflect upon the various scriptures where the God of Heaven is asking, requesting and even imploring those to whom he is speaking that they would **"listen"** to him. Sadly, there were many then who turned the deaf ear to information that God was willing to share. Is it any different today? Sharing the words of this song depict the same scenario. For those who love music, the recording of this song by Josh Groban is fantastic!

**"They would not listen
They're not listening still
Perhaps they never will..."**

"Vincent (Starry, Starry Night)"

Lyrics by Don McLean

Starry, starry night
Paint your palette blue and grey
Look out on a summer's day
With eyes that know the darkness in my soul
Shadows on the hills
Sketch the trees and daffodils
Catch the breeze and the winter chills
In colours on the snowy linen land

Now I understand
What you tried to say to me
And how you suffered for you sanity
And how you tried to set them free
They would not listen
They did not know how
Perhaps they'll listen now

Starry, starry night
Flaming flowers that brightly blaze
Swirling clouds and violet haze
Reflect in Vincent's eyes of china blue
Colours changing hue
Morning fields of amber grain
Weathered faces lined with pain
Are smoothed beneath the artists' loving hand

Now I understand
What you tried to say to me
And how you suffered for your sanity
And how you tried to set them free
They would not listen
They did not know how
Perhaps they'll listen now

For they could not love you
But still your love was true
And when no hope was left inside
On that starry, starry night
You took your life as lovers often do
But I could have told you Vincent
This world was never meant for one as beautiful as you
Like the strangers that you've met
The ragged men in ragged clothes
The silver thorn of bloody rose
Lie crushed and broken on the virgin snow

Now I think I know
What you tried to say to me
And how you suffered for your sanity
And how you tried to set them free
They would not listen
They're not listening still
Perhaps they never will...

About the Author

Roger Setterdahl is a grain and livestock farmer who owns and operates a farm near North Henderson, Illinois. Born in 1941, he attended college before joining the US. Army in 1966, spending 12 months of active duty in Vietnam during 1967_68. He and his wife Carol have two grown children. Writing is a pleasure for him, and of special interest besides farm topics is that of Christianity and religion. Participation in a small_group Bible study with friends led to the formation of TAG Ministries Foundation, Inc. This not_for_profit organization was formed in 1997 and can be located at the following web site: **www.truth_about_god.org.**

Besides this book, **"Just Between You, Me, and the Fence Post,"** the Author has written and published **"Digging Ditches, Ph.D."** and **"The Ditch Is Just As Deep On Either Side of the Road."**

Enjoy!

Note: The net proceeds from the sale of this book will be used to enhance the efforts of TAG Ministries Foundation, Inc.

Special Heartfelt Thanks

Fred M. Rogers of Mr. Rogers' Neighborhood was a man of many talents, not the least of which was composing songs. My first book entitled: "Digging Ditches, Ph.D." contains Mr. Rogers' song "Won't You Be My Neighbor?" That is one of his songs that I find myself humming from time to time. I would like to think that God would also be inclined to sing a similar song as he asks others that same question: "Won't You Be My Neighbor?" I would like to have presented a copy of that book to Mr. Rogers personally, but he died previous to publication of my book.

This book (my third) that I've written contains mention of Mr. Rogers again. In recent times, several recording artists have sung versions of Mr. Rogers' songs. This recording is available on a CD entitled: "Songs from the Neighborhood." Those artists include: Amy Grant, BJ Thomas, Bobby Caldwell, CeCe Winans, Crystal Gayle, Donna Summer, John Pizzarelli, Jon Secada, Maureen McGovern, Ricky Skaggs, Roberta Flack, and Toni Rose.

As a tribute to Mr. Rogers, Dennis Scott wrote the words and the music to the last song on the CD entitled: "Thank You For Being You." That song is written on the next page of this book. The words to that song speak volumes. As you repeat the words to yourself, perhaps you can find yourself singing those words to Mr. Rogers too, and it is even possible that you may find yourself singing those same words to God also. I do.

Thank You For Being You

Thank you for caring and helping us grow
Sharing ideas that we needed to know
But more important for all that you do
Thank you for being you.

Thank you for helping us stand on our own
Thank you for bringing the world to our home
Music and stories that we never knew
Thank you for being you.

Words can never measure
A gift would be too small
But more than any treasure
We love you most of all.

Thank you for giving your heart and your mind
Thank you for being a one_of_a_kind
You are our neighbor and friend through and through
Thank you for being you.

Words can never measure
A gift would be too small
But more than any treasure
We love you most of all.

Thank you for making us feel right at home
You made us feel special
Now see how we've grown
For all of the dreams that you helped to come true
All of the memories, too
Thank you for being you.

Words and Music by Dennis Scott
Copyright 2004 Auntie Beeb's Music

Thank You, God, for being a one_of_a_kind
Thank You For Being You.

Reference Page

TAG Ministries Foundation, Inc.

http://www.truth_about_god.org.
email: tagministries@truth_about_god.org.

Other books by the Author:

"Digging Ditches, Ph.D."
    ISBN: 1_55395_242_1
                 Trafford Publishing
                 Victoria, B.C. Canada
                     www.trafford.com

"The Ditch Is Just As Deep On Either Side of the Road"
    ISBN: 1_4120_3082_x
                 Trafford Publishing
                 Victoria, B.C. Canada
                     www.trafford.com

Other suggested books:

SERVANTS or FRIENDS? Another Look at God.
Can God Be Trusted?
        by A. Graham Maxwell

The Seven Habits of Highly Effective People.
        by Stephen R. Covey

Sun and Saddle Leather
        by Badger Clark

The Tipping Point
Blink
        by Malcolm Gladwell

Printed in the United States
by Baker & Taylor Publisher Services